OAKHURST

OAKHURST

THE BIRTH AND REBIRTH OF
AMERICA'S FIRST GOLF COURSE

Paula DiPerna & Vikki Keller

FOREWORD BY SAM SNEAD

Walker & Company
New York

First published in the United States of America in 2002 by
Walker Publishing Company, Inc.

Published simultaneously in Canada by Fitzhenry and Whiteside, Markham, Ontario L3R 4T8

For information about permission to reproduce selections from this book, write to Permissions, Walker & Company, 435 Hudson Street, New York, New York 10014

Images on the pages noted have been reproduced from the following sources: pages ii, 4, 30, 50, 53, 54, 58, 84, 87, 88, 104, 110, 115, 116, 122, 131, 149, 150, 156, 165, and 167 appear courtesy of Oakhurst; page 14 is used with the permission of the Minneapolis Institute of Arts; page 16 is used with the permission of The National Gallery, London; pages 44 and 106 appear courtesy of The Greenbrier; page 67 is used with the permission of St. Andrews University Library; page 71 appears courtesy of Colonel David Schnakenberg; pages 125, 127, 136, 143, 155, 159, 168, 169, 174, and 176 appear courtesy of Vikki Keller; page 153 appears courtesy of Cupp Design, Inc; pages 177, 178–79 are used with the permission of Cary Corthron, Lighthouse Photography.

Library of Congress Cataloging-in-Publication Data

DiPerna, Paula.
    Oakhurst : the birth and rebirth of America's first golf course /
Paula DiPerna and Vikki Keller.
        p.   cm.
    Includes bibliographical references (p.).
    ISBN 0-8027-1371-8 (alk. paper)
    1. Oakhurst Links (White Sulphur Springs, W.V.)—History.
2. Golf—West Virginia—History.   I. Keller, Vikki.   II. Title.

        GV969.O29 .D57   2002
        796.352'06'875488—dc21
            2001055904

Visit Walker & Company's Web site at www.walkerbooks.com

Book design by M. J. DiMassi

Printed in the United States of America

2   4   6   8   10   9   7   5   3   1

Dedicated to the Human Love of Landscape

Contents

Foreword:
The Flower Nobody Saw

SAM SNEAD

I HAD NEVER HEARD of Oakhurst when I was a boy, even though I lived close by on the same property where I live now, and the Montagues were still living when I was growing up.

Golf was still pretty new too, when I got started in it. By the time I was seven years old, in 1919, I was hooked on golf, but still I never knew anything about what had been going on at Oakhurst until much later. I'm glad kids today will be able to hear about Oakhurst. Most young kids don't care about the past. They want to get to the future. I don't blame them, but if you love golf, the Oakhurst story is the key to the lock.

Everything has to start somewhere. I got my start in golf caddying for pennies, when I was only a little boy. Later I helped build the third green at the Homestead. I was pushing a wheelbarrow and working on it when I was about fourteen. I was a club maker too, just like Fraser Coron, who made the Oakhurst clubs. I even met him once. I got so I could tune a set of hickory-shafted irons with a pocketknife so that the flex was similar in each club. That was a kind of art.

But of course, to play, you need at least two things— practice and talent. Some people have a little better touch than others. I say to some people I've tried to teach, "Can you swing a little slower on your backswing?" and they have no idea what to do. I've seen people who have all the talent in the world, but they don't want to practice. They will stay right where they are. Talent and desire—you need both.

I used to love hitting with hickory clubs. I'm sure that growing up in the hickory-shaft era really helped my tempo and swing. In the wood-shaft days we used hickory and maple, and when you took a swing, you had to wait to feel the clubhead come into impact. I had to put wooden shafts into iron heads. I'd have to trim them down. Some were a little larger than others, some were stronger. You'd have to go through maybe a hundred shafts to get a good one.

But comparing these clubs to today's clubs—now we are talking about comparing the Model T to modern race cars.

The most difficult aspect of hickory clubs was fixing

them—that's where a lot of golfers should start, so they can appreciate what the club is supposed to do. I remember before I went on the tour, working at the club repair shop over at the Homestead, and people would come in from someplace who hadn't played golf in a long time, so they were dying to get to the course. And if their clubs were wood, then they would have dried up and the shaft would be rattling in the metal socket. These guys would come in and say to me, "Hey, can you do something with this?" and I knew that if I put the club in a bucket of water for a half an hour or so it would swell up and get tight again. But they wouldn't wait—they were so impatient to tee it up. So, with those people I'd say, "Just a minute," and I'd go in the back, and if nobody was looking, I'd hit the club with a ball-peen hammer and give it back to them, and they'd say, "Boy, that was fast." I wouldn't have wanted to be there when the next guy tried to fix that club—it would never have come out once I got through whacking it.

Of course, once I really started playing, I didn't do those kinds of things anymore. I became the pro at the Greenbrier in 1937, and I guess I had heard of Oakhurst by then. I know I was over there hitting golf balls across the hills in 1938. You couldn't really see the fairways anymore, but I knew there was a golf course there somewhere, though I didn't know Lew Keller yet.

Golf is the hardest sport of all, I think. You have to

have so many different shots—uphill, downhill, sidehill. A guy has to have imagination. As kids, we did. We made our own homemade golf course in our backyard. And for clubs, we used any kind of wood we could attach to a steel head. Using wooden clubs makes you slow down a little bit more, think more about what you are doing.

That's where Oakhurst comes in today. Oakhurst is golf as it once was. And it's important for anyone who loves the game to understand where it all came from, how it has changed.

So if you go from a great modern golf course, like Pinehurst, to play Oakhurst, you'll say, "Boy, now I know what those guys were thinking about when they first started playing golf."

To be able to say, "I've played the first course in America"—just think what that means. It's like getting an autograph from the guy who did play that first course. It's unique.

Oakhurst was the flower nobody saw. Now everybody can see it, just as it was when it was born, and when golf was born in America.

OAKHURST

PROLOGUE

SOMETIME IN 1879, an American named Russell W.
Montague picked his way on horseback through the
crackling woods of West Virginia until he reached an expanse of open land. Contoured, shapely, an island of
space in a sea of trees and cascading hills, the land was
called Oakhurst. Montague decided on the spot he had to
own it, though golf was nowhere in his mind then.

He was beguiled by the Greenbrier region as soon as
he relocated there with his wife and infant son from
Boston, to try his hand at farming. His intent had been to
escape dirty urban air and the practice of law, since he
had very little wish or drive to be a lawyer.

Montague was a Boston Brahmin who could trace his
ancestry back to William the Conqueror's days in England, but he left those traditions behind. He could never
have planned that his chosen path to happiness and satis-

faction would also lead him to preside over the first transplant of golf to the New World, nor that America's first full-fledged nine-hole golf course, Oakhurst Links, would come to exist on his land.

Golf, which had its origins in Scotland as early as the 1500s, was still generally unknown in the United States when Montague reached West Virginia. The tantalizing sport had been gathering energy and followers across the world, but its wave had yet to wash across the Atlantic and land on America.

Montague had been born in 1852 in Massachusetts, a middle son, just a few months before Lionel Maynard Torin also came into the world, an ocean away in Scotland. Torin, a second son, was born to the castle, literally, at Aldourie on the shores of Loch Ness. The Torins were of the leisure class, though not a golfing family. Young Lionel spent vacations with his parents either at the seaside in sunny Italy, or in France, at Pau. There, the senior Torin liked to hunt, but there too the first golf course in continental Europe had been opened in 1854, a successor to makeshift rounds played there by Scottish officers decades earlier. The Torins spent more than enough summers at Pau for the young Lionel to observe, perhaps even learn, the alluring mysteries of the Scottish pastime.

While Montague wrestled with how to avoid a predictable legal career as a young man in Boston, Torin traveled the world. His journeys landed him in faraway Ceylon (now Sri Lanka), where he became a tea estate manager. There, he joined only the best gentleman's clubs, including what would become Ceylon's first golf club. Lionel Torin also became one of Ceylon's first golfers.

Torin and Montague would likely never have met, let alone played golf together, had it not been for another aristocratic and wayward Scot. George Grant, Torin's elder cousin, for reasons lost to history found himself living in the Greenbrier Valley next door to Montague. A middle son, Grant had sought his fortune and his freedom in America. However, when he came to live in West Virginia, he certainly couldn't have foreseen that he would soon host his globe-trotting cousin Lionel, whose reputation as an excellent and fervent golfer preceded him from Ceylon, on an extended visit.

Building a golf course in the middle of nowhere to entertain a dashing young relative might have seemed outlandish to most men of the time and setting. Grant, though, had made friends with his neighbor, and Russell Montague's home had by then become a focal point of other distinctly Scottish entertainment, for Grant had lured two other Scotsmen, Alexander and Roderick MacLeod—like him, not first sons, from a prominent neighboring family in Scotland—to try their hand at frontier living in Greenbrier. The MacLeods had bought a farm overlooking Montague's, so many a cold night

Russell W. Montague

found these four men sitting around Montague's fireplace, singing Scottish ballads, drinking Scottish whisky, and wondering, most likely, what would be the next twist in life so many thousands of miles from home.

As it happened, these men would be key characters in the annals of golf history, laying out America's first organized golf course on Montague's land and playing America's first real golf games there, using America's first real golf clubs, made by Montague's carpenter, who became, in turn, America's first golf-club maker. The Oakhurst friends would create America's first golf tournament and first golf prize, amusing themselves for years in a hidden corner of America, while virtually no one else knew.

The five men who gave birth to the nine-hole Oakhurst Links played it happily in splendid isolation for about a decade until their adventure in America came to an end. Eventually the Scots headed back to Ceylon and Scotland, and Montague was left alone to wrestle with life in the modern age.

Gradually wildflowers and clover overtook Oakhurst Links; the fairways and greens slowly disappeared. Meanwhile other golf courses began sprouting up around the country, for by the turn of the century, golf had begun its march to become one of the most popular distractions ever known to man or woman.

The original Oakhurst Links would have probably stayed lost forever had its saga not intersected, through pure happenstance, with the life of a golfing legend, Sam Snead. When he was born nearby in 1912, the course had already grown over into scruffy pastureland. It was even more ragged in 1938 when Snead, then a renowned golf pro, hit a golf ball for the fun of it across Montague's old fairways.

Snead eventually met and became the lifelong friend of a younger golf devotee and businessman named Lewis E. Keller. And it was Snead who tipped Keller off that Oakhurst might be for sale. Keller fell in love with the Oakhurst property as swiftly and surely as Russell Montague had some seventy-five years earlier. In 1959, the day he first saw it, Keller bought the land on a handshake from Montague's only living heir.

The Oakhurst golf course would slumber for several more decades while Keller raised racehorses there. Yet Oakhurst Links kept whispering to him. A bit more than a century after it was first laid out, Oakhurst Links was reborn, brought back to playable life in 1994 by Keller, friends, and renowned golf course architect Bob Cupp. Meticulously, they unearthed the original layout, lovingly restoring the playing conditions of the nineteenth century on the eve of the twenty-first.

The modern player can thus experience the scale, dimensions, and feel of the game at the beginning of its American history. Oakhurst imports replica clubs and balls of the original Oakhurst period made in Scotland, and only these are used to play. Golf carts, even golf bags, have no place, and the thrill of hitting a ball cleanly 100 yards is the thrill of hitting a truly long shot, by 1880's definition.

Oakhurst Links is not a theater or a simulation, but a real-time access to an experience long since gone. As such, it is unique in the world; Oakhurst Links has never known the modern game. Here the art of golf cannot be found in the gloss of new equipment or million-dollar prize money. At Oakhurst, the game at hand is exclusively the game within, divorced from every modern pressure.

The complete story of Oakhurst has never been told. It is a tale of ingenuity and desire, of American history meeting golf history. It is the recovered saga of what can happen when passion comes together with place, and the passion is a royal and ancient game.

1

HOW GOLF LEFT SCOTLAND

ALL GOLF GAMES are part dream. Anyone who stands over the first shot of the day has already conjured the result in the mind's eye, and heard a contact as clean as the snap of a dry twig as the ball takes flight in a certain undying arc across a peerless sky. All golfers dream of playing beautiful golf, and they keep coming back because the quest is always as near and as possible as the next chance to play. Russell Montague was one of these.

In 1852, the year Montague was born in Dedham, Massachusetts, due east across the Atlantic Ocean, at the legendary seaside at St. Andrews, Scotland, a new jet-black steam locomotive chugged against the taut sea wind along a rambling stretch of hallowed ground known as the Old Course. It was inauguration season for the first railway link between the ordinary outside world and a royal and ancient world of devotees and diehards.

The earliest golf games were played in Scotland at tiny medieval St. Andrews. The game grew out of the primeval geology of the Scottish coast and sea, and became inseparable from the coastal comb of sand and grass that had gradually become, by invention, play, decree, and then widespread public habit, the venerable Old Course. All golf courses in a sense have derived from this setting: The Old Course at land's end has become the reference point of all play thereafter.

The railway completed in 1852 was a pet project of the provost, Sir Hugh Lyon Playfair, surely a felicitous name for a man with golf as his mission. The fastidious Playfair was so dedicated to the improvement of the town that he insisted on being rolled around in a rickshawlike chair by a city clerk so he could spot disorder and have it tidied up.

Sir Hugh had also been busy fighting the ocean as it sought to steal back the land it had given up. To protect the edges of the fairways at the Old Course against the eroding forces of high tides, Playfair ordered the building of three breakwaters. They were fortified by landfill built from the public garbage that Playfair loathed, which was covered with sand and soil brought from inland.

Playfair had wielded the clout of his office for a decade, and his dogged beautification plans began to pay off with the advent of the railroad. It soon brought so many golfers and holidaymakers that the eighteen holes of the Old Course, where golf had been played for uninterrupted centuries, no longer sufficed to meet the burgeoning Victorian demand for amusement and escape. Golf at St. Andrews would never be the same.

৯

ST. ANDREWS HANGS ON the coast at the mouth of the river Eden, a lucky stretch of land constantly lashed into salty wounds by the busy North Sea, yet never quite vanquished by its force. Instead, the constantly surging tides created the *hlincs*—Old English for land ridges left unplowed—and the flowing river inexorably transported banks of soil to the coast.

Thus linksland evolved, mounds of dune and sand carried onto the coast by wind and water, deposited like surplus, and left behind as useless. Links land is held together by sparse grass and vegetation fit to survive only in harshness. Fists of thorny gorse, as yellow as hot mustard when in bloom, spike the hand or finger. At times winds sweep the dunes to the height of modest buildings. Linksland has little farming value, no soil nutrients, an unstable shape, and severe vulnerability to rain and erosion.

As it happened, these lean tongues of unpredictable land for which humans had no conventional use made possible an unconventional vocation. The hard facts of where and when golf actually began are lost in at least five centuries of debate, argument, and mystique. As golf scholar and writer Robert Browning explained in his classic work *The History of Golf*, establishing the truth of golf's origins is not as easy as looking it up in an irrefutable encyclopedia. The task is more a matter of piecing together snippets of history and far-flung sources and commentary. Browning noted that a prior writer had remarked in 1890, "To write the history of golf as it should be done demands a thorough study of all Scottish Acts of Parliament, Kirk Sessions records, memories, and in fact, of Scottish literature, legislation and history from the beginning of time.... A young man must do it, and he will be so ancient before he finishes the toil that he will scarce see the flag on the short hole at St. Andrews from the tee."

However, for those who don't want to make a life's work of golf history, there are a few undisputed touchstones. One of the earliest written references to the game came in 1457, in an act of the Scottish parliament. King James II had felt obliged to outlaw the playing of golf because he was concerned that his troops were so enamored of the game that they were spending more time perfecting their golf shots than keeping watch on the realm.

This was an era of intense rivalry between the thrones and royal families of Scotland and England. In that golf clubs were produced by bow makers at the time, it is easy to understand how a Scottish king might have worried

Act of Parliament, 1457, banning golf.

that his soldiers, who claimed to be headed out to practice their archery, might pick up a golf club at the bow
maker's instead.

The first known image of what could conceivably be
the sport of golf predates the edict of King James by more
than a century. A panel set in a stained glass window in
England's Gloucester Cathedral, which was built between 1340 and 1350, depicts a male player swinging a
stick with what might be a clubhead for some deliberate
purpose resembling a golf shot. Centuries later, veteran
golf writer Al Barkow, in his book *The Golden Era of Golf,*
observed that "golf is an extension of a very ordinary in-

stinct; hitting an object with a stick to propel it is as elemental as looking to see where you are going."

It is also generally agreed that a game like golf, called *kolven*, played with an implement known as a *kolf*, was a pastime in Holland in the mid-1400s. The *kolfs* looked like golf clubs, the name sounds enough like *golf* to hint a connection, and the gist of the game was to move a ball around a field or on ice.

A cousin to this game known as *chole* was played in Belgium and northern France a century earlier. Its early depictions also resemble what we know as golf today. Browning prefers the *chole* origin to the *kolven* link. He theorizes that a group of Scottish soldiers on duty in France picked up the game of *chole* in roughly 1420. Then they brought it back to Scotland, where it rooted and evolved into a game to be played over a planned route by players in a group, each autonomous, yet all aiming to get a small ball into the same hole in the ground.

By 1502 sufficient peace reigned in Scotland that King James IV felt it safe to be seen playing golf. He bought some golf clubs from a bow maker in Perth that year. The next year James IV married Margaret, daughter of Henry VII, then king of England, a marriage intended to seal an era of peace with England. In 1504 James IV played perhaps the first royal golf game, recorded in the royal Treasury accounts, with the earl of Bothwell.

The game rapidly became a Scottish national pastime,

*The game of chole, from a painting by Flemish artist
Paul Bril in 1624.*

enveloping even women, including the embattled Mary,
Queen of Scots. In fact, it can be said that golf may have
contributed to Mary's losing her throne, and perhaps
later her life. She apparently loved the game and was seen
playing publicly within a few weeks of the murder of her
husband, Lord Darnley, in 1567. This was deemed suspiciously unmournful behavior for a mourning widow, and
it was among the evidence that led to Mary being
charged with complicity in her husband's murder; this,
and other hints of treason, forced her to flee for her life.
She took dubious refuge in England, where she was im-
prisoned for years and finally executed in 1587 by her

[14]

cousin, the dour Elizabeth I. Elizabeth had wanted to dampen any claims to her throne by rival factions, particularly Scots. Shortly after Mary's denunciation, several orders were issued banning the playing of golf during the time good citizens were supposed to be in church, or as it was put, "in tyme of sermonis."

The public's right to play golf on the links land at St. Andrews was firmly established by royal decree as early as 1552, even though the same land was also being used for pony riding, drying clothes in the sun, carpet beating, cricket, croquet, and even rabbit raising. In fact, rabbit holes are often presumed to have been the first golf holes. Still, no formal golf entities existed then, and organized golf clubs would remain unknown until the mid–eighteenth century.

Strategically situated and famous as a learning and ecclesiastical center, St. Andrews was also a thriving trading town. Many Dutch merchants came and went, doubtless also exchanging tales of pastimes and distraction. It is likely through this commercial interchange that the Dutch-Flemish experiences of *kolven* and *chole* amalgamated into the Scottish version of the game.

By 1618 there was enough demand for golf balls that King James VI of Scotland sold a monopoly for golf ball production to two merchants, James Melvill and William Berwick, to promote a new national industry. Meanwhile golf had crossed boundaries, for in 1603, when James VI

Kolven, played on the ice near Haarlem, from a painting by Adriaen van de Velde.

had also gained the throne of England, he seeded golf there too. The king and his courtiers played on open lands at Blackheath before any formal club or golf course existed there. As Browning sums it up, "From the Peace of Glasgow in 1502 to the Revolution of 1688, every reigning monarch of the Stuart line—two kings and one queen of Scotland, four kings of the United Kingdom—was a golfer."

By the late 1600s the English were so enamored with

Charles I receives news of the Irish Rebellion while playing golf on Leith Links, after the painting by John Gilbert.

golf, they were arguing with the Scots over the origins of the game. In roughly 1680, a match was played to decide the question. This was the first known international golf tournament. The Scotsman, James, then the duke of York and the brother of the king of England, Charles II, was serving his brother as emissary to the Scottish parliament. James was dared by two visiting Englishmen to prove Scottish golf superiority with the partner of his choice. The match was to be played at the links at Leith, and the duke put out the call for a golfer to join him in defending the golfing honor of Scotland. The man recommended to him by the regulars at Leith turned out to be someone well beneath the duke's social station, a poor shoemaker named John Patersone. Nevertheless, Patersone was reported to be the best golfer of his day, descended from a long line of distinguished local golfers.

The pairing proved perfect, and the duke and the shoemaker won the match handsomely. To show his pride and gratitude, the duke split the significant purse with Patersone. This amounted to enough money for Patersone to build himself a stately house in Edinburgh, right off the regal Royal Mile. The duke also had designed and affixed to the wall of the house a crest with the seal and arms of the Patersone family. To further honor Patersone's golf skills, the duke had carved into the crest the words "Far and Sure," adorning an image of a hand clutching a golf club. There were other words too—"I hate no person"—derived from the letters of the name John Patersone.

The building and insignia stood for several centuries longer, demolished only in 1960, when it was deemed a neglected tenement. Nonetheless a replica plaque still marks the spot known as Golfer's Land, in a narrow alleyway off Number 77 on the Royal Mile in Edinburgh.

The Patersone tale proves that while kings and queens loved golf, in the early days the game was also a sport for all social classes. This egalitarian flavor contributed to the worldwide spread of the game. Scottish workers of all trades took golf with them wherever they went, particularly Scottish bridge builders, whose skill in engineering was renowned.

As the British Empire expanded, so too did golf. By 1829 the Royal Calcutta Golf Club had been formed in India, followed by the Bombay Club in 1842. Somewhat later, in time for Lionel Torin's arrival, golf reached Ceylon, another outpost of British activity. There are no first-hand descriptions of golf in Ceylon from Torin himself, but the game there definitely had its oddities, according to reports of the time. Caddies dressed in not much more than a handkerchief to cover the groin, and on some occasions, out of sight of the players, they laughingly imitated gestures and ritual, including the waggle of this or that aristocrat during the setup at the tee.

Being far from home only appears to have exaggerated the zeal players had for the game. Golfers in Ceylon set out in any weather, including just after a drenching rain, chasing balls out of ditches, drenching their gentleman's white-duck suits in mucky red mud, and risking the breaking of an ankle or leg in the maze of hidden crab holes that dotted the playing area along the sea.

Local workmen had no real idea how to produce golf clubs. In Ceylon, players often found the clubs they'd ordered from a local woodworker had shafts as thin and whippy as fishing rods, limp against a golf ball, because the craftsmen simply had no conception of what they were supposed to be making.

&

BY 1880 GOLF HAD traveled across many continents. It was known in Europe, Australia, East Asia, New Zealand, Hong Kong—even at the tip of South Africa—and as close to the United States as Canada, where there were five golf courses by 1876. Yet only hints of the game had appeared in America during this time.

An early reference to Scottish golfers in America dates from 1779, when some soldiers played in New York during the Revolutionary War, keeping up the tradition of soldiers wanting their golf clubs handy. The golf market thrived enough for the king's printer in the colonies, James Rivington, to run a side business in golf clubs and balls for royal troops. He teased them with promotions, suggesting that, "the Season for this pleasant and healthy exercise now advancing, gentlemen may be furnished with excellent clubs and the veritable Caledonian balls, by enquiring at the Printer's."

Golf, or a similar game, perhaps *kolven* or *chole*, though called "golf," had been played in the Dutch-American colonies raucously enough to be outlawed in Albany, New York, as early as 1659. Authorities claimed they had heard diverse "complaints from the burghers of this place against the practice of playing golf along the streets, which causes great damage to the windows of the houses, and also exposes people to the danger of being injured and is contrary to the freedom of the public streets."

The first reference to golf in a publication in the United States appears to have been in 1772, according to *Golf Journal,* the publication of the United States Golf Association. Benjamin Rush, who would sign the Declaration of Independence, included a reference to golf in his "Sermons to Gentlemen upon Temperance and Exercise." Of golf he wrote, "An exercise which is much used by Gentlemen in Scotland. A large common in which there are several little holes is chosen for the purpose."

Surviving printed invitations to dinners and dancers prove that a golf club existed in Savannah, Georgia, as early as 1796; it appears to have died out in 1818. But there is no record of there having been a golf course, or even a few rough-hewn golf holes, in Savannah at that time. This club may well have been simply a social club for golfers who may never have played more than random shots.

There is no doubt that a similar social golf club had been formed in Charleston, South Carolina, by 1786, with a clubhouse on Harleston's Green, modern-day downtown Charleston. A shipment of 96 golf clubs and 432 balls had been sent to Charleston in 1783 from Leith—the venerable golfing site of John Patersone, the shoemaker-hero. They were addressed to Scottish merchants John and David Deas, whose father was a shipowner in Leith. While the assumption can be made that with so much equipment reaching the area, local devotees played golf on Harleston's Green, there is no record of a golf course having been laid out there, or even any formal holes having been configured; nor did any formal golfing event take place. John Deas died in 1790, also leaving no record of what he might have done with all those clubs and balls, and the history of the Charleston Golf Club petered out.

Thus, prior to 1884 golf, though a pastime on far-flung continents, had simply not taken firm root in America. American golf remained a matter of dots that had not been connected, and there was no organized approach to the sport. However, in that year, the game Scotland had given the world arrived in the isolated hills of West Virginia.

2

A FINGERTIP ON THE MAP

RUSSELL W. MONTAGUE was not expected to live a long life, though he certainly came from stalwart stock. An extensive Montague family genealogy, published in 1986 but compiled over several generations, traces Montague's roots as the family's European and American history gradually entwined.

The name Montague, also spelled de Montagu, de Montacuto, or Montacute, as in the Latin, appeared early in human history. One of the earliest was Drogo de Montagu, who was born in A.D. 1040. He became a friend and follower of Robert, the earl of Moriton, who was the favorite brother of William, the duke of Normandy, soon to invade England.

Luckily for Drogo, who joined William's audacious expeditionary army of sixty thousand men and three ships, the invasion in 1066 went splendidly for their side.

William the Conqueror rewarded those who had helped him take over England with vast tracts of English land. Drogo's reward included several manors in Somerset County, complete with a castle crowning a hill named after him and built in his honor by his friend, Robert the earl. It was so commanding a spot, a writer described it as a "noble mount" shaped like a cone, topped with a tower and open balustrade from which a "flag is occasionally displayed floating 56 yards in the air and exhibiting a grand and picturesque appearance."

For the next five hundred years, the Montagues lived and worked in the company of kings in and out of power. In 1337 William Montacute, a direct descendant of Drogo, was granted the title earl of Salisbury, and this earldom carried the Montague name to the generation that set off for America in the 1600s, when it passed through marriage and various twists of heritage out of Montague hands.

The first descendants who set sail for America were Peter Montague, who landed in Virginia in roughly 1634 with his wife, and his brother Richard, who turned up in written records in 1646 in New England. Richard and his wife eventually settled in Connecticut, and one historian noted, "At an attack of Indians, Richard Montague was impressed to make a supply of bread, and his horse was taken by a trooper."

The Montagues in America were farmers and traders

and pub keepers and blacksmiths, and by the fifth transatlantic generation, the American Montagues were firmly established in the reputable class. The family embraced the American Revolution, and at least one member, Seth Montague, enthusiastically poured boxes of tea overboard at the Boston Tea Party. He saw the revolution through to the surrender of the British commander, Lord Cornwallis, which he witnessed as one of George Washington's officers.

The first family member to graduate from a New England college was the Reverend William Montague, born in 1757 in South Hadley, Massachusetts. He was Russell Montague's grandfather, a pillar of entrepreneurial stock and also a rebel at heart.

According to the family history, William started his professional life as a carpenter's apprentice, but while he was learning this trade, the British Army invaded the United States from Canada in 1775. The young Montague saw the war as his ticket to the world beyond South Hadley, and hoped he'd be drafted during the call-up to reinforce the American troops in the Massachusetts area. When the master carpenter for whom he worked received his notice to report for duty, William eagerly offered to take his place, since the Continental Army held that one draftee was as good as another. William's parents, reluctant to let their son go, relented when a family friend and colonel promised he'd keep the boy safely under his wing as an orderly. Thus, William's wartime service was mostly free of battle. Though he saw several encounters, he was off duty when the British general Burgoyne gave up his sword to the American northern army at Saratoga, New York, in 1777. William nonetheless watched the ceremony seated atop a fencepost within earshot of the somber but triumphant proceedings, another Montague to witness a full-dress British surrender.

The family record further recounts that when William returned home from the war, he announced to his family that he would not be returning to carpentry but was heading off to Dartmouth College. When his father protested that the family did not have the financial wherewithal to pay for this elevated learning, William set out anyway. He stuffed some clothes and provisions in a cloth knapsack, along with the soldier's wages he had saved, and walked across Massachusetts to Hanover, New Hampshire, some two hundred miles through woods and rugged byway. He eventually put himself through college by doing odd jobs, falling back on his early experience with hammer, nail, and carpenter's plane. He graduated second in his class, took a job for a time at a school for girls, and then studied divinity. He soon landed one of the key clerical spots in the American Episcopal church, rector of Christ's Church in Boston.

William Montague went on to become one of the foremost clergymen in New England. He married Joan

Little, of equal Yankee pedigree, in 1801 and became the rector of St. Paul's church in Dedham, Massachusetts. Russell Montague was born in 1852 to one of their sons, George, and his wife, Catherine Prescott, the seventh generation in this stalwart New England clan.

The little that is known about Russell Montague's childhood derives from an account written much later by his granddaughter, Harriet Wellford, sometime in the 1960s. The memoir is a key source of information on the life of Russell Montague and his involvement with Oakhurst Links. Harriet Wellford recounts that her grandfather, being the thirdborn, struggled to distinguish himself from his older brothers, William and George. When he was nine years old, Russell went so far as to rig a pendulum mechanism in his bedroom. He got it to swing without stopping for three days and nights, and then proclaimed that he had invented the elusive perpetual motion machine, though the pendulum stopped soon thereafter. Of this incident, Harriet Montague would write, "Russell Wortley Montague was always something of a dreamer."

Russell's parents, unlike his grandfather's, could afford the costs of higher education, and Russell entered Harvard University as a member of the class of 1872. The Harvard he experienced was hardly a luxurious place. There were only dirt paths across Harvard Yard, which turned to mud in any forceful rain. Dormitory halls were unheated, and the tiny private bedrooms drew warmth from the large fireplaces below through tiny grates in the floor. The grates also served as stoves for heating hot water in a saucepan or cooking pot. Students had to carry clean water to their rooms from a pump in the yard, to bathe in a basin or a bucket. As one observer of the time wrote, "It is very probable, especially in winter, the students looked cleaner than they really were."

In 1872 there were twenty-three teachers in the whole of Harvard College, with 114 members in Russell's graduating class. There is no record of Russell's academic standing, save that he earned a stern warning from the faculty that he might not graduate because he was failing history. He also managed to be "privately admonished," as the school records put it, for absence from recitation—cutting class—as well as for missing prayers. It can also be gleaned that Russell had a frisky side at Harvard, for he was fined two dollars for "cutting seats" in a classroom when he was a junior.

The sports opportunities at Harvard in Russell's time were by today's standard very limited. An Englishman visiting in 1871, Thomas Hughes, found the offerings rather meager, as he described in an article for the magazine of Oxford University, his alma mater. As if assigned to dissect truly foreign ways, he wrote, "Want of a bathing place is only one of many signs of the indifference to a variety of pastimes which soon strikes an Englishman at Harvard.

Cricket has been noted too tedious and is not, I believe, played at all. The same may now be said of foot-ball, for a certain annual collision between Sophomores and Freshmen, on a day known as Bloody Monday, has brought out an ordinance against the game. So baseball, a game almost identical with the 'rounders' of our schools, enjoys undisputed pre-eminence among land sports. The Harvard Nine have reached a high degree of excellence in this national game, as many Americans love to call it, and they are said to be superior to any club in the States, except perhaps the professional White and Red Stockings. I do not deny that the game is a good one when well played, but frequent accidents are caused to hands and knees by the violence with which the ball is thrown to the bases and it has not a tithe of the skill or variety of cricket."

Russell did earn his bachelor of arts degree in 1872. His first foray into the working world was as an assistant teacher in a private school, and some months later he took a job in a Boston law firm to learn the legal profession.

Just as he had followed his brother William to Harvard, Russell also followed him to live off campus in Chelsea, a pretty town on the northeast side of Boston Harbor, which had begun to flourish as a fashionable resort for Bostonians. Russell, a somewhat pudgy but dapper young man, soon came to know the daughters of a leading Chelsea family, the Carys, for William had boarded at 34 Parker Street, otherwise known as "Retreat." This was the

Russell Montague at Harvard.

ancestral home of the Cary family, which had been rent-ing out rooms to make ends meet. William had married Helen Cary in 1872, and in August 1874 Russell Mon-tague married her sister; his wife, Harriet, was thirteen years older than he.

Though he had entered the Massachusetts bar that same summer, Russell decided to put off actually practic-ing for a time. He chose instead to travel with his bride to England, ostensibly to polish his law skills in London at the famous legal inns, England's crossroads of law offices and courts. It is not known whether Russell actually gained useful legal expertise while in England. However, there is some evidence that the six months he and Harriet spent in the British Isles were enough to introduce him to the royal and ancient game of golf.

THE EARLIEST REPORT of Oakhurst Links appeared in 1913, years after America's first golf course ceased operation. Florence Flynn visited Russell Montague in his West Virginia home for an article in *Golf* magazine. According to Flynn, Montague "had played at St. Andrews and a number of the other clubs in the old country." Presumably, Montague had provided this information on his first exposure to the game. There were a handful of golf clubs in England in 1874–75. The closest to London was the Royal Blackheath Golf Club, established in roughly 1766, the first club in England, founded by Scottish exiles. By 1844 the club had incorporated a competitor and moved to Eltham, a few miles from London. Montague may well have learned about golf at these London settings, introduced by London friends.

No record exists of Montague having played on the Old Course at St. Andrews, but the course has never kept an archive of every round and player. Then, as now, anyone could play without entrée or membership in the Royal and Ancient Golf Club. The Old Course has always been utterly public, the proverbial village green, open throughout the year except on Sunday.

It is unlikely that Montague would have chosen to visit St. Andrews during the winter of 1875, for that year the weather was so fierce, walls of snow stopped the Playfair trains dead on the tracks. More plausibly, Montague, perhaps with his wife too, would have gone to St. Andrews for the start of the official season in May. Play was inaugurated by the annual meeting of the Royal and Ancient Golf Club, and heralded by the local newspapers as "a welcome break in the dull monotony of life."

On May 8 that year, at eleven in the morning, a cannon shot burst across the first hole to signal the start of the club's first formal round of the season. The top score of the day was 102, shot by a Captain Fordyce, in a setting described by a local columnist: "The pellucid waters of the ocean murmuring in his ears, the yellow bloom of the gorse fringing his course, and the fresh green fields beyond, it is no wonder that the golfer, who is also a lover of nature, should be attracted to St. Andrews to pursue the game over the links."

Later that week, the young Montagues may have seen a sharp-edged match pairing the legendary Toms, Tom Morris and son, surely the most famous golfers in the world at the time. "Old Tom" Morris had been born in 1821 in St. Andrews and had become one of the first professional golfers, having started his career as a club maker, apprentice, and devotee of great players of his day. He was also a pioneer in turf science, serving as chief superintendent at St. Andrews for forty years, where he introduced such innovations as lining the putting cup with metal so it would not lose shape in the ground. Young Tom, born in

1851, just a year before Montague and Torin, was a true golf natural who had won his first golf match at age thirteen. He then swept the tournament scene, winning the British Open four times before his untimely early death at the age of twenty-four on Christmas Day, 1875.

But that spring, the Morrises turned in a match of top-notch skill. They pushed three holes up on their opponents, dropped four holes in a row, then came back to take the match by seven holes, with a joint score of 85. The crowd was thrilled.

The Montagues might also have stood among the "large and brilliant asssemblage of spectators" watching a tournament of women players, women having had a club of their own at St. Andrews since 1867, with "the number of competitors considerably greater than in former years." In 1875 twenty pairs of women competed in the first match of the season, with the winning gross score of 102 shot by a Mary Simon. This means she was every bit as sharp and as credible a competitor as Colonel Fordyce, who had played a few days earlier, there being no difference in the game men and women played on the Old Course with respect to distance and par.

Montague's golf mentor is unknown, but it could have been just about anyone in English society, considering the extent of the Montague and Cary networks. Indeed, if the Montague name was well known in America, it was truly famous in England.

Lady Mary Wortley Montagu, a relative through the English Montague branch, had been one of the most recognized raconteuses and writers of the eighteenth century, as well as a medical pioneer. Russell was also related to the family that held the earldom of Sandwich. In fact, it had been the insatiable gambler John Montagu, the fourth earl of Sandwich, who in the mid-1700s changed the English lexicon and menu forever by inventing a way to eat and play cards at the same time. He ordered his attendants to place pieces of meat between bread slices and keep them on hand, literally, so he could eat without having to put down his cards to wrestle with knife and fork.

At some point during Montague's stay in England, according to his granddaughter, he visited a physician, who declared him of frail constitution and recommended he choose to live somewhere salubrious and restful and far from urban grit. Thus, in mid-1875, Russell and Harriet headed back to America. Montague's granddaughter recorded what has become basic Montague family lore: While shipboard at sea, Russell opened a map of the United States, his physician's advice fresh in his ears, and perused the chart to plan his future. His finger came to rest far from Boston and New England and all that Montague stock had come to know over centuries and generations—on tiny West Virginia.

THE REGION MONTAGUE had fingered had once been so wild and unknown, early cartogaphers simply termed it "the endless mountains." Today the hills are still blanketed by humid, moist forest that blocks, then subtly admits, the sun, playing tricks with light and moisture.

The Greenbrier River was probably first mapped by French Jesuits in the late 1600s and named Rio de Ronceverte, River of Green Brier, for the tangled dark forest all around. The river was first encountered by white settlers in 1749 at a time when to be an explorer meant little more than setting out with a single musket and a buckskin sack of survival sundries into an America whose western boundaries were entirely unknown.

At first, relations between the white settlers and the Native Americans of the region, primarily the Shawnee, went fairly well. A chronicler of the time wrote that the Shawnee were "often among the whites, appeared friendly and were received without suspicion." However, the rate at which the whites took Indian land eventually brought on war, and the Shawnee fanned out in raiding parties. An infamous massacre took place at Muddy Creek in 1763, led by a chief named Cornstalk.

By 1778, though Greenbrier County had been formally established, there was still no road in the area wide enough for a wagon or cart. There wouldn't be one until 1782, when Virginia became one of the original thirteen United States. The separate state of West Virginia would not exist until almost another century had passed, when it separated from Virginia proper.

In addition to tobacco, the settlements of the Greenbrier region exported bacon, maple sugar, cheese, wool, beeswax, feathers, tallow, poultry, hemp, ginseng, cattle, and butter, and towns began to thrive on trade, though still surrounded by true frontier. Soon, as America's hunger for building grew, lumber became a valuable commodity, and the Greenbrier region slowly began to prosper on the western edge of the new nation.

As timber and woods were cut to make way for human settlement, rich, verdant bluegrass sprung up where there had once been forest, ideal for livestock, including horses. Greenbrier bluegrass was a bonanza, so rich in protein and minerals as to rival the more famous bluegrasses of Kentucky.

Nonetheless, though Greenbrier County in the late 1700s ought to have been able to develop full-blown livestock and agriculture industries, at the time the frontier economy had not yet fully engaged. Very little cash was available for investment, and it appears that the settlers lacked the necessary competitive edge. Anne Royal, an observer visiting the area, wrote in 1826, "From everything I have seen of these people, they lack every requisite essential for commercial purposes. . . . Their peltry trade heretofore has been valuable, and ought to have yielded an immense profit, but from their want of commercial knowledge, they always have been and still continue to be the dupes of the merchants. . . . They are without capital, system, or enterprise, nor do they seem ambitious of either."

Russell Montague himself observed, according to his granddaughter, that all he accomplished in his first stint as a lawyer after returning by ship from England was to improve his chess game. He freely admitted keeping a chess set in his bottom desk drawer to pull out whenever he had the chance. Indeed, nothing suggests that Russell Montague ever took his legal career seriously.

It is not clear exactly when the newlywed Montagues headed south to the West Virginia region Russell had conjured on his voyage home. Their first child, a son named Cary, was born in Massachusetts in 1877, and it is likely they set out soon after that. However, how they managed to travel through the wilderness with their newborn son has escaped all family record.

Harriet Montague, Cary's daughter, makes scarce mention in her memoir of the trip from Boston, other than to say it took weeks by train and wagon, and that Russell and his wife covered the last forty miles on horseback as far as Glencoe, where they apparently did live for a time. They were certainly settled in White Sulphur Springs by 1878, for their second child, Margaret Prescott, was born there that year.

On the trip back from England, as he considered how he might earn a living outside the legal profession once back in America, Montague had met a group of young sons of Scottish and English families. Their parents were paying five hundred dollars a year to unspecified Americans to teach these idle gentlemen some real skills, like farming. On the voyage, his granddaughter reports, Russell toyed with the idea of presenting himself as a dairy expert to his fellow travelers to earn the five hundred dollars, but thought better of it. He would, it turned out, be a soft touch himself for a farming swindle soon after reaching the Greenbrier area.

A memoir written in 1915 by William Bowditch, a budding landscape architect who had come to the Greenbrier area and thus to know Russell Montague through a friend in the early 1880s, describes Montague's first agricultural adventures. Bowditch recorded that Montague had "run against a Mr. Lawrence, also of Boston . . . who was a visionary, impracticable creature, who had never raised a sheep in his life but had acquired certain book knowledge of the business." According to Bowditch, Lawrence used his "wonderful 'gift of gab'" to interest Montague in sheep farming, though "it transpired that Lawrence knew nothing whatever about the business."

Bowditch guessed that Montague threatened to sue the smooth-talking Lawrence, but "it was no use."

In any case, Russell was not ready to give up on farming yet. According to his granddaughter, he took to raising pigs on his second try, on leased land, but his hired hands spent most of their time stilling and swilling moonshine. When the pigs came down with cholera, his farmhands quit. Montague's farming future seemed doomed.

[39]

Nonetheless, if Montague could not make any money at animal husbandry, neither could he bring himself to move away from the enchantment of Greenbrier's glades and hollows. One day he came upon the parcel of land called Oakhurst.

Some landscapes bring together shape and curve and light in a feeling of perfect assembly. Oakhurst must have been like this, as it still is today—meadows surrounded by woods, nourished by flowing creeks, exuding calming silence. Montague may have leased the property at first, but in February 1880 he became the owner of the 640 acres that would enfold and captivate him the rest of his life.

❧

THE LAND AND FARMHOUSE were situated about three miles from the town of White Sulphur Springs and a hotel known as the Old White, which would eventually become the Greenbrier resort.

According to the hotel's official history and other documents of the time, the hot-water pools of Greenbrier County were known to its earliest settlers, the nomadic Powhatan Indians. They suffered from sore feet and rheumatism, but kept their cure to themselves—sulfur waters they drank and bathed in. Later the Shawnee, seeking the source of the salt lick where their game congregated, traced it to a marsh whose pungent aroma was carried on the breeze to them well before the waters came into view. Gradually, it is believed, the Shawnee began to understand that the sulphuric waters had curative powers.

According to the local histories, during a lull in the warlike mood around Greenbrier, in 1778, the Shawnee revealed the existence of the waters to one settler with whom they were friendly, a rheumatic Mrs. Anderson. She persuaded some friends to carry her on a cot fifteen miles to the springs so she could try the Shawnee remedy. Her friends hollowed out a tree to make her a bathtub and filled it with hot water and heated stones to hold the water's warmth, as the Indians had recommended. Mrs. Anderson bathed and drank, and her pain disappeared almost entirely after some weeks.

In fact, White Sulphur Springs were one of about a dozen mineral springs in the area, collectively known as "the springs of Virginia." These included the famous Hot Springs of Virginia, where Thomas Jefferson had been one of the earliest patrons, and others with salubrious names like Blue Sulphur, Sweet Springs, and Sweet Calybeate.

By the 1820s, even though the area had just barely acquired its first stagecoach route, word had spread, especially through the southern states, that something special existed in Greenbrier County. Cottages and other guest amenities sprang up, and taking the cure became fashionable. Diplomats, plantation moguls, foreign dignitaries, congressmen, writers, artists, and simply the idle rich began to congregate at the Greenbrier springs. Henry Clay, one of the early prominent visitors, then speaker of the House of Representatives, spent three days at the springs in 1817 with one servant and three horses and paid $16.50 for his stay, exclusive of his personal bar bill. In the early heyday, those with social entrée could happily mix with the likes of Dolly Madison, Daniel Webster, Davy Crockett, and Francis Scott Key.

In 1857 the guest facilities at White Sulphur Springs were sold to a group of prominent Virginians, who felt that the political climate was stable enough to warrant a significant investment in the resort industry. They raised an elegant and unprecedented structure the next year, naming it the Grand Central Hotel, but it was immediately nicknamed the "Old White" by habitués for its brilliant white colonnade entrance. It dwarfed any hotel in the nation at the time, and capacity jumped from six or seven hundred guests to nearly sixteen hundred by 1860.

When the Civil War broke out in 1861, both the Union and the Confederacy fought bitterly for the strategically situated Greenbrier area. The Old White itself, which the owners had rented to leaders of the Confederacy as a hospital and headquarters, flew the Confederate flag. General Robert E. Lee, who had vacationed at the resort in the 1840s in unencumbered times, now found himself on guard in Greenbrier around the once gay grounds.

During the war, antislavery sentiment brewed in the

region. Abolitionists seized the moment to build upon the long-standing frustration of several local counties with the central Virginia government. They declared the new antislavery state of West Virginia, which was officially proclaimed by President Abraham Lincoln in 1863. The newly incorporated Union state included Greenbrier County, even though most sympathies in the county lay with the Confederate cause.

The Old White survived the war. In 1868 the Chesapeake and Ohio Railroad network formed, and a stop was established in White Sulphur Springs. The refurbished Old White became the only resort in the springs area with direct service to its gate from the main cities of the country. The picnics, cotillions, and restorative baths resumed in earnest.

There are no records that Russell Montague ever set foot in, much less frequented, the stately corridors and ballrooms only a few miles down the road from Oakhurst in the years after he bought the property. He certainly had the social pedigree that served as the ticket for entry, but he may not have wanted to spend money on frivolities, for he had enough demands on his finances.

Montague's granddaughter wrote about Russell's ongoing struggle to reinvent himself as a farmer and his purchase of Oakhurst: "My grandfather's investment was not inspired by business principles so much as by the view from the Oakhurst porch. From it, one could see seven

The Old White in the 1880s.

ranges of mountains stretching off in the distance. Most of the 640 acre tract was not good farming land . . . and when crops did succeed, they were more a source of surprise than income."

Another Montague relative observed, "Uncle Russell stands on the porch and manages Oakhurst with a megaphone in one hand and his wife's checkbook in the other." Montague was clearly ready for distraction.

3

A FOURSOME WAITS
IN THE VALLEY

FAMILY RECORDS DO NOT reveal how Russell Montague first met the transplanted Scotsman George Grant. However, by the time Montague had purchased Oakhurst, Grant already owned a large estate, Greycliffe, just a few miles down the road.

Grant's family hailed from northern Scotland in Morayshire, an area commanded by the town of Forres. The ancient settlement is perhaps as old as Ptolemy, who according to legend may have marked it "Varris" on a map more than two thousand years ago.

Shakespeare, too, knew this rugged beautiful region of Scotland, where the Firth of Moray, a large bay, glistens occasionally in the sunlight but is more often lost to the human eye in the cool, wet fog known locally as the harr.

Shakespeare traveled to Morayshire to gain inspiration for *Macbeth*. The drama opens on a Morayshire heath, where the nobleman Banquo asks three withered witches, "How far is 't called to Forres?"

In 1800 James Peterkin, a prosperous merchant who had been doing business in the British Caribbean colonies, bought an expanse of land in Forres and built an imposing gray stone mansion a few miles from the coast, large enough to bespeak status, yet small enough to feel nestled in the woods. The home, finished in 1805, was named Grange Hall, and when Peterkin died in 1812, he left the estate to his son, John. When John died, Grange passed on again to Mary-Anne, his sister, the next and only rightful heir. She later married Major Peter Grant, owner of the adjacent estate, Invererne.

Peter Grant was considerably older than his bride and a dashing British military man fresh from service in India. Since Mary-Anne Peterkin would not have inherited Grange had there been a living male Peterkin heir, she inherited the property on condition that she retain her family name so that it would not die out. Thus, when Mary-Anne Peterkin married, her new husband added her surname to his, becoming known as Peter Grant Peterkin. He rented out Invererne and moved into Grange, and they began their family immediately with the birth of a son, James, and soon after two more children—a girl, Anne, the youngest, and George, born in 1839.

When Russell Montague was just learning to walk in America, the fifteen-year-old George Grant Peterkin had his portrait painted, one thumb hooked into a blue velvet vest, wearing a blue-black velvet bow tie. The painting would hang in a trio with portraits of his siblings above the sweeping central staircase at Grange.

George left Grange for boarding school and entered Emmanuel College at Cambridge University in 1860, as his elder brother, James, had done a few years earlier. He excelled not so much in academics as in rifle competitions, major sporting events of the time.

George's family eventually purchased him a commission in the British Army, that being an acceptable way for the British government to augment its defense budget and for gentlemen to become officers. He joined His Majesty's Forty-fifth Regiment of Foot, which, having begun in Robin Hood's Nottinghamshire, took the name the Sherwood Foresters in 1866. By then George had purchased the rank of lieutenant. Drawing on his expertise as a marksman, he became the regiment's instructor of musketry for two years. He shipped out to India with his regiment in 1864 and had several tours of duty there. By 1868 he was back in Scotland, very likely on sick leave, as many soldiers in his regiment had been stricken with cholera and other fevers. In 1871, at age thirty-two, George turned his back on army life, selling his commissions in time to be home for Christmas.

On the death of his father in 1878, Grange Hall passed to George's elder brother, James. Dividing ancestral property was to be avoided at all costs, and primogeniture dictated that the full wealth of Grange would pass out of George's reach. He did, however, inherit the nearby, less grand house, Invererne. He might have gone to live there had he not been caught in a cloud of community disgrace over a love affair with his sister's governess. Whether the ensuing public scandal became an ugly public storm he had to escape, or whether he simply lacked the courage to marry the woman and hold his ground, the events were enough for him to leave Morayshire.

How Grant traveled to America is not known. However, in March 1879 he was not only living in Greenbrier County, West Virginia, but also filing a name change. He dropped the Peterkin surname altogether in a formal legal announcement, recorded in 1879 and also published in the *Times* of London: "I intend henceforth to use only the surname of Grant and be known, and in all legal and other documents describe and sign myself as George Grant."

There are several inconsistent secondhand versions of Grant's first days in West Virginia. Montague's son Cary wrote that Grant, while serving in the British Army, had developed "what was then known as 'India liver.'" This version continues that upon Grant's return to England, "he was advised by the best of the medical profession that he could not live very long, but that if he went out to Virginia and led an open air life, he might last two years. In a despondent mood, Grant spread out a map of Virginia, shut his eyes and stuck a pin in it. The pin landed at Covington. Following what seemed to be his destiny, he went to Covington and there heard of White Sulphur Springs, twenty miles further over the mountains. Upon his arrival

George Grant

at White Sulphur, he was so pleased with the nature of the country, that he immediately bought what was then known as the old Cowardin place, in the Big Draft."

Cary Montague also wrote that Grant was "a man of considerable means and very energetic. He bought up thousands of acres and went into a lumber business and his health steadily improved. After some years, he built a modern brick house on part of his land and named it Greycliffe. I have been told that this residence had the first bathroom in Greenbrier County."

This account, with Grant randomly fingering a map to find his fortune, also in response to a doctor's admonition that he ought to reside in a healthy clime, does sound suspiciously like Russell Montague's own tale, and could well have been mixed up by the grapevine of posterity. However, Grant's army records do show he had suffered from ill health during various periods of his army career. At home in Forres there was a fabled establishment known as the Cluny Hydropathic Institute, and Grant may very well have heard about America's healthful sulfur springs through contacts at Cluny.

In any case, Grant apparently knew as little about farming in America as Montague, for another account that mentions Grant's first Greenbrier days, the letter written by Nathaniel Bowditch, describes Grant as a friend of Montague's early enough to have also been a victim with him in the Lawrence sheep swindles. Bowditch, who had also met Grant, further observed that Grant's "habits were not wholly above reproach, though his sprees had a periodicity to them that enabled his friends to know when to expect a debauch and, in a way, prepare for it."

Grant had actually owned land in the region as early as 1872, though what or who led him to these early investments is not known. In fact, Russell Montague himself had bought some land from Grant shortly after he arrived in the White Sulphur Springs area to round out his holdings, though it is not clear which man was the first to actually live in the area.

❧

GRANT HAD NO DOUBT sent word of his success and pleasant new surroundings home to Forres; by 1880 two other Scotsmen had arrived in Greenbrier to live nearby, the MacLeod brothers, Alexander and Roderick. Their ancestral home in Scotland, Dalvey Castle, was barely a few miles from Grange, and they bought a tract of land on Bob's Ridge overlooking Montague's property, on which they built a house. Like Grant and Montague, they were not the first sons in their family. Their eldest brother, Norman, had inherited the historic family home and title of laird of Dalvey in 1876 at the young age of nineteen. A journey to America might have greatly appealed to Alexander and Roderick, who were twenty-two and twenty respectively when they arrived in Greenbrier, joining Montague, who was twenty-eight at the time, and Grant, the elder statesman at forty-four.

Thus four men came to live next door to each other in a region to which none of them was connected by family, lineage, or any logical root, yet which had lured them to live out some level of personal adventure.

❧

BY THE TIME the MacLeods reached the area, Russell and Harriet Montague were well established there. In

Alexander MacLeod

May 1879 Helen Cary, the sister of Russell's wife, Harriet, and the wife of his brother William, had visited the young Montague family in Greenbrier. She wrote her aunt back in Chelsea that the region was "delicious, calm, inspiriting and refreshing . . . you never *imagined* so many mountains. I haven't the powers of description. I can only say I have never had such a day of enjoyment of scenery as yesterday, so elevating and satisfying . . . the mountain views are utterly lovely and the soft air, though cool, does not give any cold."

In the early 1880s roughly 15,000 people lived in Greenbrier County. Lewisburg, a few miles away, was the

Roderick MacLeod

nearest major town to Oakhurst and White Sulphur Springs. When the Chesapeake and Ohio Railroad had been completed, not only did the Greenbrier resort have a new lifeline to guests, but products from West Virginia could move in any direction across the frontier. Business in Lewisburg hummed along in a variety of establishments.

Russell continued to refer to himself as a farmer. He had been buying up additional parcels of land since his arrival, amassing fields and woods but not doing much to improve them, other than planting some fruit trees up on Bob's Ridge, near where the MacLeods lived. There fruit, especially peaches, seemed to do well without much tending. Gradually, Montague's welcoming farmhouse had become the gathering point for his neighbors, Grant and the MacLeod brothers, but amusements were not plentiful. Electricity had not yet reached Greenbrier then, though the first central power station in America had begun operating in New York City in 1882.

According to Montague's granddaughter's memoirs, when the temperature dropped below freezing during Greenbrier winters, many a night would find the fire roaring at Oakhurst, with Montague hosting the local retinue. Oakhurst became the hub of ambling fireside conversations and elaborate games of charades, and even productions of Shakespeare's plays—*Macbeth* among them, doubtless a gesture to the Forres roots of the Oakhurst Scots—complete with sound effects. For when the line, "Thrice the brinded cat hath mewed," was spoken by one of the grown-ups, Montague's children didn't hesitate to yank the tail of their cat Luce right on cue. In fact Alick and Rod MacLeod became so familiar to Russell's son, Cary, and his daughter, Margaret, that the children considered the jovial Scotsmen to be their own best friends.

On these fireplace evenings, Alick MacLeod in particular would sing old Scottish ballads with abandon, play his bagpipes, or recite verse of his own creation, dubbing himself "Ye Hereditary Bard of ye Alleghenies." One of his stanzas has survived: "Ye kine of Weste Virginia, once roamed ye shaded delles, of emerald hue, where Montague on his broad acres dwelles."

While Russell was married with children and thus had responsibilities, Grant and the MacLeods were bachelors, drawing comfortable sums from home and local holdings to support their expatriate living. There is no record of what the MacLeods ever farmed, other than some fruit, and George Grant most certainly would have been termed a "MnPlsr"—the official local census abbreviation then for "Man of Pleasure." His fortune was banked, his estate house built, and his leisure time unbounded.

❧

SOMETIME IN THE EARLY 1880s, George Grant got a letter announcing that his cousin Lionel Torin, until then manager of a tea operation in Ceylon, was coming to Greycliffe for a visit. Torin had been born at Aldourie Castle, just south of Inverness, and shared the birth year of 1852 with Russell Montague. His father, Richard, was English and he had married a Scottish lady, Amelia Isabela Fraser-Tytler, and fathered Lionel at age fifty-three. Aldourie no longer stands, but was only a few miles southwest of Forres in Morayshire. Torin's mother was a relative through marriage to the Grant Peterkins—an intertwining of lineage critical to the Oakhurst tale, for it is hard to otherwise imagine how Torin would have been drawn to distant Greenbrier County.

Torin's family were well established and of Huguenot descent. According to a family history compiled by Torin's nephew in the 1930s, the Torins had fled to England in the late 1600s, like other French Protestants before them, to escape persecution by the pope and the French Catholic kings. The family was prominent enough in their flight to have had a bridge—the Pont de Torin—and some coastal rockscape—Les Roches des Torins—named for them in France, near Mont-Saint-Michel.

The Torins took their place in the English aristocracy as well as in the military. Lionel's father was born in Bombay, as Lionel's grandfather had been for many years with the East India Company, where he had been known as a crack cricket player. There is no record of the Torins playing golf, but they would have gotten close to it in India at the time, for the Royal Calcutta Golf Club, established in 1829, boasted the first course in the world outside the British Isles.

Golf could have also come into Lionel's life via the door of France. Despite their persecuted bloodlines, the English Torins still liked to travel in France, and Lionel's parents were continental in their habits. When they weren't summering in Scotland by the lakes, they were wintering in their villa in Posillipo, near Naples in Italy,

Lionel Torin

or in the hunting lodges and inns in Pau, just north of the Pyrenees Mountains in southwestern France.

The first golf course in continental Europe had opened at Pau in 1856, a nine-hole layout founded by Scottish military officers on holiday. In fact, legend has it that two Scottish officers played makeshift rounds at Pau even before there was any official course, as early as 1814. They reportedly packed golf clubs with their military gear in case there was a lull in the ongoing battle against Napoleon in the theater known as the Peninsular War.

In 1871, at the age of nineteen, Lionel Torin—having by then completed a world tour with his brother Ernest that included stops in Russia and South America—decided to put down roots several oceans away from Scotland, in Ceylon. He joined the classic British gentlemen's club, the Colombo Club, that year, its first year of existence. The clubhouse had been built in the shape of Noah's Ark on downtown Colombo's Galle Face Green, a broad expanse along the seafront. By 1874 Torin was managing the Glenlyon Estate in the Dimbula district of the island. Coffee was king at the time, with tea just coming into its own. Four years later, the twenty-six-year-old Torin had become coproprietor of Ceylon's Aldourie Estate, named for his mother's ancestral home and birthplace.

Golf finally came to Ceylon in 1880, when the Royal Colombo Golf Club was established in the capital city, the first meeting having been held at the Colombo Club premises in 1879. Torin was not among the Golf Club's founding nine members, but he had been one of the earliest members of the Colombo Club proper. Certainly the denizens of one club were likely to become habitués at the other.

If not, for there is no record of Torin's earliest golf days, his golf leanings might not have needed an official golf setting in which to flower. Aldourie Estate, which Lionel co-owned, had 270 acres in 1878, of which 214 were cultivated in coffee or tea. However, 9 acres were described simply as "cultivated grass" by the surveyor then, a somewhat mysterious and surprisingly uncommercial use of

[59]

land on hard-pressed tea estates of the time. The grassy area may have been a croquet field, but there is another possibility. Early in 1878, Lionel had visited his brother Ernest, who was then stationed in nearby India, where golf was widely played. Lionel could well have laid out some personal golf holes at his tea estate on his return.

Sometime between 1880 and 1884 Lionel Torin decided to leave Ceylon for a while, possibly because the coffee blight was in full sway, laying waste to plant after plant. Entire estates went bankrupt, with nothing to export. Tea was planted en masse to try to interrupt the spread of the burning blight, a switch that tipped Ceylon toward tea growing from then on.

The long journey to Greenbrier County would not have daunted Torin, and once arrived, he would have quickly met the MacLeods and Montagues and been woven into their lives. As Russell Montague's granddaughter Harriet put it in her account, "Mr. Torin was one of the many stray Englishmen who came and went between the old and new countries. In those days, when travel was more difficult, a visit often meant six months to two years. Of course, summer guests at the Springs stayed only three months, but that was long enough to vary the monotony of the Montagues' days. In fact, each person who entered their lives became an event."

In this case, the event transcended the man. Lionel M. Torin brought his golf clubs with him.

4

THE BIRTH OF OAKHURST LINKS: GOLF MAKES BETTER GOLF

THOUGH IT IS UNCLEAR how Lionel Torin acquired his reputation as a golfer, there is no question he had one, for it sufficiently preceded him to give pause to his host, George Grant. As Florence Flynn wrote in her 1913 article for *Golf* magazine, Grant knew that "time would hang heavily" for his golfer guest if there were no links.

Among the group, only Russell Montague had land that was relatively open, with natural slopes and elevation. In fact, Montague had acquired the thirty-five acres on which Oakhurst Links would be built from Grant some years before. As for golf experience, there is no record that Grant or the MacLeods ever played golf in Scotland, but they were certainly born in its aura—one of the game's very earliest courses existed as early as 1672 just four miles from Forres, at Burgi. Playing golf in America would not have seemed outlandish to any Scotsman. And for Montague, a man who governed his land from his porch, who chose to situate himself not for profitability but for the seduction of the view before his eyes, who had sheep on his property he had never truly known what to do with, and who may well have had some golf memories of his own, building a golf course for his friend and neighbor would have made perfect sense.

❧

HISTORY IS NOT CATEGORICAL as to the exact origins of the Oakhurst golf project. Torin may have arrived as early as 1881, as recorded by the great golf course architect Charles Blair Macdonald in his 1928 book *Scotland's Gift: Golf.* "There is evidence," he wrote, "that in 1881 a couple of miles west of White Sulphur Springs, W. Va., a few holes were laid out and half a dozen men played golf." Florence Flynn's 1913 article for *Golf* magazine, the earliest known article on Oakhurst, says Torin arrived in 1884 and does not give a specific date for the founding of the golf course. However, in June 1914 an article without a byline appeared in the *New York Times,* titled "America's Pioneer Golf Course at White Sulphur Springs," which refers to an 1882 origin for Oakhurst. The *Times* piece, rather shamelessly paraphrased from the 1913 Flynn article—perhaps she herself recycled the earlier magazine work for the newspaper—also claims that "Mr. and Mrs. Montague placed their estate at the disposal of George Grant and a number of their English and Scottish neighbors when the latter told them that the Oakhurst acres would make an ideal course"; it states that Grant and Torin laid out the course in 1882, and that "a couple of years passed before it was in perfect condition." Montague's son Cary cited 1884 as the starting date in his brief account of the evolution of Oakhurst, titled "The History of Golfing in the Greenbrier Valley and Its Spread Throughout the Country."

Russell Montague himself noted 1884 as the date for the founding of the Oakhurst Club in an interview he gave in 1936 to Forrest Jackson for *Rail* magazine, and he would have provided the information for both Flynn's piece in 1913 and the 1914 *New York Times* article.

The uncertainty may also derive from another detail in Cary Montague's version of events. He wrote that Torin and Grant first "made a little three hole golf links on the 'Greycliffe' grounds," and that later the links were "laid out on the Oakhurst property and consisted of nine holes." The precursor course could well have failed at Greycliffe, for that is one of the few flat plains in Greenbrier, and is situated where the slightest rain would have easily turned a fairway to mud. Oakhurst, on the other hand, drained beautifully, and Montague had become familiar through his attempts at farming with irrigation, soil content, absorption, layering, and other agronomical details that he could have drawn upon when the course was taking shape.

Yet another account, published in 1929 in the *American Golfer* and written by Innis Brown, who also interviewed Russell Montague and visited Oakhurst, says Grant, Montague, and the MacLeods laid out the course to prepare for Torin's arrival, and that "by the time Torin arrived, there was the golf course."

What is undisputed is that by 1884 the Oakhurst coterie was actively playing on a course of their own making. They lost no time in organizing themselves into a club and declaring themselves the only members. As Montague would put it later in *Rail* magazine, "The Oakhurst Club was a very small one."

༂

THE NOTION OF A formally planned golf course was alien to the sport in the 1880s. Thus Montague and his friends had no models in golf course design to follow, and the eventual layout of Oakhurst Links was based on instinct and trial and error, much as were golf courses in Scotland. In one of the earliest essays on golf design, written in 1889, crack British player and writer Horace G. Hutchinson observed, "Up to a certain point, no rolling or mowing is so beneficial to the levelling of putting green and course as the tread of the human foot. Golf makes better golf. If you could get a regiment to mark time for a week on your worst putting green, you would, at the end of that time, probably find it your best."

The earliest golf games had been played in Scotland in distinctly natural spaces, the Old Course at St. Andrews—which appears to have existed in some playable form as early as 1414—exemplifying the original idea that the golfer created the course as a function of playing the game. Early golfers would have picked their way over the ancient dunes and mounds, spotted an enticing target ahead—an indentation in the links or some feature that invited a ball to land—and declared that a golf hole for the day. The number of holes in a round varied with how many such targets the players found in the land as they went along, with the original Leith course offering only five holes, and another early course at Montrose as many as twenty-five.

Golfers logically favored the lower, greener areas; hence the origin of the fairway. However, linksland redefined itself constantly as dunes shifted, turning a green area, for example, into sandy scrubland over night. Also, since linksland was fully public, grazing livestock too had the right to be present. Sheep, especially, burrowed into the same spots, wearing out the thin grass to reveal bare sand and create the earliest bunkers. Likewise, the holes

and tunnels of rodents and game, like rabbits, would col-
lapse now and then, opening up new places to lose a golf
ball. Thus, the course played one day could be unfamiliar
terrain the next.

For centuries, the holes at St. Andrews had been
played as nature set them out, along a very narrow neck of
land shaped like a shepherd's crook, nowhere more than
forty yards wide, with eleven holes running end to end. In
1764, believing some holes too short and crowded, the
club members agreed to compress the first four holes into
two, leaving nine out and nine in, thereby making the
eighteen-hole round the touchstone layout thereafter.
Nonetheless, even Alister MacKenzie, the renowned golf
course designer who collaborated with Bobby Jones to
create Augusta National, home of the Masters, had difficulty in discerning the logic behind the Old Course. In
1923 he wrote that the order of the holes was very likely
the work of "someone, perhaps, who had heard of the
game and went cutting holes three or four hundred yards
apart on attractive plateaus, where long white feathers
stuck in holes would be visible, until he got to the end of
the available playing area."

Even when golf play moved inland away from the clas-
sical coastal linksland in Scotland and England, golf
courses were laid out in existing public commons and
spaces, with little, if any, human landscaping. Innovations
were designed to protect the precious turf rather than

Golf at St. Andrews in the 1880s.

modify its design. For example, horses were outfitted with special leather boots so their hooves wouldn't churn up the fairways as they were mowed. The turn of the nineteenth century saw such tools as the Pattison firm's patented steel-spring flagstaff—Pattison also made the horse boots—advertised as "indispensible where cattle are grazed." The spring in the flagstick allowed it to bend when animals, including the grass-tending sheep, bumped into it or used the stick to scratch away an itch or knock off a fly. This prevented a stick from damaging the circle of the hole.

Russell Montague and his friends were decidedly of

[67]

the "golf makes better golf" school of design. In laying out the course at Oakhurst, they worked, no doubt, as the first players had unearthed the holes of the Old Course, playing their shots and declaring their holes. In this they were both dabblers in and pioneers of golf course design.

The first hole at Oakhurst was a natural. It would not have taken much golf design expertise, when sitting on Montague's front porch, to notice the opening in the woods near the pond he had been using to hold water for his crops, and to imagine siting the first hole there. A golfer's eye could have easily taken a ball high up over the water, to land just at the threshold of the dirt road that led into the property. From there a player could try to hit the ball to a green situated on a flat area on the other side of the road, just near enough to the creek to make anxious the player who hit long. The only reference to the original concept of the first hole comes from Innis Brown's 1929 article: "Immediately in front of the house was once the first tee of Oakhurst. You played from there across a small gulch onto a still higher knoll to the first green. Mr. Montague showed me the line."

There are no surviving firsthand accounts of the building of the course, though Flynn in 1913 noted that Montague's farmhands were employed in the task. However, very little work had to be done, since Montague owned enough open and contoured land to accommodate nine holes. Pacing, walking, hitting shots now and then to get a sense of feasibility, Montague and company could easily have situated the holes by following the contours of nature. The hills at Oakhurst rise and fall just enough, so golf potential was inherent in the landscape; as Flynn remarked in 1913, "The country was like a bit of the bonnie heather hills of Scotland set like a jewel in the heart of the Alleghenies." According to Flynn, who could likely still discern the outlines of the holes on her 1913 visit, the course was "ideally laid out. It stands a monument worthy of the most famous and ambitious of professionals who have laid out and developed well-known courses throughout the world."

🌹

ALISTER MACKENZIE ONCE WROTE, "The truth is that golf courses and other playing fields require grasses with a thick matted root growth and a dwarf leaf—grasses which require little mowing and provide a firm springy carpet that is a pleasure to walk on." With its bounty of bluegrass, Oakhurst met the requirement easily.

The records do not show what Montague and his friends used to cut out the putting holes on the greens, or where they had the cups, made of metal, cast into shape. Of these, Flynn wrote in 1913, "The cups still in the ground are cumbersome, thick and heavier than those used today." Byrne Bauer, a writer who also talked to

Montague, said in a 1938 article that "the fairways were pastureland where sheep roamed at will; their nibbling kept the grass clipped. The greens were sheep pasture too—clipped by their sharp teeth and were made slightly more level merely by rolling with a weighed wooden roller." It is not clear where Montague would have gotten that piece of equipment, other than by borrowing it from the Greenbrier Hotel, which may well have used a roller to keep its croquet field flat.

An article written after Montague's death claims that the Oakhurst friends did borrow a mechanical lawn mower from the Greenbrier during the construction, though there is no corroboration of this statement. However, possibly Montague's earlier friendship with Ernest Bowditch, a young landscape architect who worked for a time at the Greenbrier, may have given them access to equipment.

Bowditch in his memoir mentioned that he had to convince the owners of the hotel to upgrade their mowing equipment from an old horse-drawn Buckeye mowing machine, which was far from state-of-the-art at the time. The hotel subsequently bought so many new mowers that, Bowditch wrote, "the sound of them was audible from daylight to dark," because many of the grounds hands wanted a chance to push one for the fun of seeing the grass blades fly. Thus, quite possibly, the golfers at Oakhurst were able to either spirit away one of these new-fangled mowers or simply borrow the cast-off Buckeye.

The first and slow gears being bevel gears, and the second and fast gears being straight, or spur gears, there is no wearing out of gears, no lost motion, no loss of power by vibration, no noise. The Buckeye furnishes

The Most Motion with the Least Friction . . .

. . . The Most Work with the Least Effort.

BUCKEYE MOWER.
SHOE-SLIDE AND LEADING WHEEL.

The Buckeye Mowing Machine.

And so they began, the first golf games in America played over a designed piece of terrain, by five men with such a yen for a game they built their own golf course in the middle of the woods. In the words of Florence Flynn, "The Montague place was admirable for golf links and, the first in the States, was the sportiest to be had."

5

FAR AND SURE

THOUGH THE 1914 *New York Times* article speaks of regular friendly matches and states that "the players were handicapped and scores were kept from year to year for classification and record," no scorecards or other written accounts of play survive at Oakhurst. As for the length of the original course, there is no absolute certainty. The best information is that which Montague himself could remember in 1938, when he told Byrne Bauer that the course was between two thousand and twenty-five hundred yards long. Match play was the main format of the day, and the rules that would have applied during the Oakhurst heyday were still very much the game's earliest rules.

At its origins in Scotland, golf had no rules to speak of; however, as the game became popular, these became necessary. Once competition among strangers had become commonplace, courtesies among friends could no longer be relied upon to resolve playing disputes. Thus, in roughly 1754, leading golfers of St. Andrews drew up basic "Articles and Laws in playing the Golf." No marking of balls, or removing of obstacles, was permitted, and a ball stopped by "person, horse, dog or anything else" had to be played wherever found. If a club broke during the backswing at address, a stroke was nonetheless counted. And even then, there was no sympathy for lost balls: "If you should lose your ball by its being taken up or any other way, you are to go back to the spot where you struck last and drop another ball, and allow your adversary a stroke for the misfortune."

These basic rules, somewhat refined during the succeeding 130 years, would have been the applicable guidelines during the Oakhurst period, including the stymie rule. This nagging regulation required a player to play around anything in the way, including and most especially on the putting surface. Balls in the way could be lifted only if one was touching the other. Marking the ball was not yet acceptable. And if a golf ball cracked, split, or broke outright during play, the player had to play the largest piece until holed out.

Broken golf balls presented more than a score problem to the Oakhurst players; how to replace them in a country that didn't even know what they were was a greater challenge. Indeed, lack of golf equipment threatened to end the Oakhurst golf adventure before it got started. At first the group had only the clubs and balls that Torin had brought along. Fortunately, Montague soon remembered that Fraser Coron, a handyman on his farming payroll, was a skilled woodworker who had carefully carved the pews in the little church nearby on Big Draft Road, Montague's own place of worship. Montague immediately introduced Coron to a new line of work—copying Torin's golf clubs so the players could have a steady supply.

At the time, most wooden clubs were the long-, or needle-, nose type, long from heel to toe, and they looked more like hockey sticks than today's clubs. Players acquired them one at a time, and there was no such concept as a matched set. The clubs were slender and fragile, and there was no source from which to buy any in America.

Coron, born in 1854 in Greenbrier County, converted his carpenter's workshop to a club maker's den, going to work with a lathe he had used for shaving the spokes of wagon wheels and a hand knife. He copied the few clubs on hand at Oakhurst, no doubt supervised at first by Torin, who likely had had his share of experiences in Ceylon with clubs so thinly whittled they bent like a fishing pole. Quickly, America's first golf course gave birth to America's first golf-club maker.

Fraser Coron found his supplies in the ample woods and fields around Oakhurst, primarily apple and hickory, flexible but tough. He cured the apple wood in a kiln, cut

Needlenose drivers made in the 1890s.

it into a rough block, and then sculpted it with finer tools into a narrow golf-club head. He carved the shafts from hickory wood, fitting them to the clubhead so the faces and grooves lined up perfectly, then wound them together tightly with fishing line and other strong twiny material.

Coron's workshop also no doubt reeked of vinegar, for he had to soak bits of ram's horn in a vinegar solution to soften it. Thereafter he could carve the horn into a plate to set into the sole of the club to provide weight and strengthen the club for clean contact with the ball. Coron also became expert in working leather, needing well-cured strips for the grips of the clubs. These were cushioned with wool, of which there would have been plenty at Oakhurst, along with ram's horn. At last Montague's hapless try at sheep raising had found a use. At the same time, Montague and company realized they needed to open a private route from Scotland for golf equipment, for Coron

[75]

couldn't supply all their needs. Early in the life of Oakhurst, Montague wrote a friend, George M. Donaldson, seeking help in this endeavor. Donaldson had been born in Scotland in 1850, married an American woman, Sallie Ould of Richmond, in 1882, and had land interests and a lumber company in Virginia. He traveled to and from Scotland regularly, and was delighted to serve as golf club purchasing agent. As requested, he would bring back from Scotland a cache of clubs to add to the Oakhurst supply. Montague, in turn, invited him to become the sixth member of Oakhurst Links.

In his 1929 conversation with Innis Brown, Montague recalled that "in those days, not one man in a thousand had ever seen a golf club, and we had some right funny experiences getting them into the country." According to Montague, on one trip, when Donaldson stepped off his ship in America, his precious cargo was seized. Just before he got through customs, the odd shapes in his luggage caught the eyes of a zealous and suspicious inspector. Montague observed, with some delight no doubt, "The customs inspector had no idea what the clubs were and was very suspicious of them; said they looked like some kind of long-handled blackjack or other deadly weapon to him. So he had them sent to Washington for classification and a ruling, and it was some weeks before poor Donaldson got them."

The clubs eventually made it to Oakhurst, none too

soon. Coron by himself could not meet the needs of six men, who no doubt broke a lot of wooden clubs with aggressive swings and erratic timing.

Golf clubs of the time were further stressed by a shift in golf ball technology that had taken place some thirty years before Oakhurst was founded. Until about 1850, golf balls were called "featheries," and were made entirely by hand in an elaborate process as demanding as sewing silk. Bits of leather were stitched into a sphere and a small opening left so that the leather skin casing could be turned outside in and the ball stuffed. Feathers from various fowl had to be boiled ever so carefully to get maximum softness, then pushed through the tiny opening. The ball maker had to use a metal spike to force the feathers into the fragile orb without tearing it apart, an action not unlike trying to force feathers into an eggshell through a pinhole. In 1838, Scottish records suggested a master golf-ball maker could produce only about fifty featheries a week.

The featheries were as feisty to play as they were difficult to make. Golf aficionados in Glasgow, conducting an eighteenth-century version of a ballistics test, found in 1786 that the average player could hit a feathery roughly 200 yards—a surprisingly long distance. Indeed, in 1836 a Frenchman named Samuel Messieux, who had

Feathery balls made by John and William Gourlay.

won the Royal and Ancient Gold Medal in 1827, is said to have driven a feathery ball 360 yards on the Old Course, a feat of somewhat superhuman prowess regardless of the century.

On the other hand, the featheries got soggy in wet weather and were apt to fall apart, not to mention being wobbly as they rolled, throwing plenty of putts exasperatingly off line. Given that feathery balls could be produced only at the pace of hand-sewn artwork, and that the increasing number of players created an insatiable demand for golf balls, the golf world was forced to come up with a better model.

Golf technology, following the lead of other industries, reached into the tropical forest for a solution. Guttapercha, the oozing sap of the sapodilla tree family (*Payena* spp.), which grows in rain forests in Asia, has remarkable characteristics: endlessly malleable when softened in hot

[78]

water, it hardens into toughness when cooled. Ancient gutta trees in the nineteenth century stood eighty feet tall and grew to a diameter of four feet. The tapping technology used at the time was crude: trees were simply cut down to get at the bark, strip it, and extract the juice.

Gutta-percha had unlimited potential as the Industrial Revolution spewed out patents for new products and gadgets. In addition to being malleable, gutta-percha was advantageously portable. Once the sap was heated to remove resins, it solidified as it cooled. Thus exporters in Asia, where the British had plenty of export-import business already under way, could send it to Europe in neat blocks, rather than messy vats. In Europe the material became known as "mazer wood." And it was melted and molded into all manner of products, including whip handles, paper cutters, hollow piping, stethoscope tubing, storage bottles, book covers, wire insulation—it did not burn—and even dentures.

The story has entered golf lore that a poor boy named Robert Paterson, son of the Reverend Robert Paterson, who lived in St. Andrews, introduced the gutta-percha golf ball. In 1845 his family had received a statue of the Hindu goddess of fertility, Vishnu, from another son who was living abroad as a missionary. The Vishnu figure had been packed in sheets of gutta-percha for safe travel, and the financially strapped Paterson family kept this packing in case they might have some purpose for it later.

Rob, the son, soon figured out a use. Those were dark economic days in Scotland, and the cost of repairing shoes was out of reach for a modest household like the Patersons'. Rob's shoe soles were wearing out, so he decided to melt some of the family's gutta-percha cache in a pot and spread it across the bottom of his shoes, where it solidified in place. The process yielded perfectly serviceable soles that withstood the rough cobblestones of St. Andrews so well that Paterson had a second revolutionary idea. There was another necessity he couldn't afford—golf balls—so he melted down more gutta-percha, and as it cooled, he rounded it out in the palm of his hands, like a chef fashioning meatballs.

The story is told that Paterson played with these hard homemade spheres, which he also painted white, on the Old Course at St. Andrews in 1845. When they broke apart, which was often, Paterson took the pieces home, melted them down again in hot water, and remolded them back into shape. When they cooled, they were ready for his next round.

Some golf histories report that another of Paterson's brothers refined and improved his creation, cooking off impurities and removing recalcitrant air bubbles. On the other hand, golf historian Robert Browning ascribes credit for the gutta-percha golf ball to the W. T. Henley Telegraph Works Company, which had mastered gutta-percha through the experience of using it to insulate underwater telegraph cable. In any case, word of the "guttie" ball's prowess spread from St. Andrews on the golf grapevine. Reportedly by 1848 the leading feathery maker of the day, John Gourlay, took up making gutties and never looked back.

The gutties were by far more durable than featheries, and they were also half the price, putting golf one step closer to becoming a mass-market game. In addition, gutties were a major step toward the industrialization of what had been a sport dependent on handmade, one-of-a-kind equipment. Until then the golf club had been an implement of art, an all-wood expression of grain and tone interpreted through the eyes and hands of individual club makers. Uniformity had been unachievable.

During the reign of the feathery, iron clubs were heavy and crude and bruised the feathery's leather casing. Iron clubs were used mainly to play balls out of wagon ruts or other difficult situations. Declaring an unplayable lie was still a source of confusion, even affront, to the rule makers, who were struggling at the time to define what made a ball unplayable.

With the gutta-percha ball, much tougher than the featheries, and with improvement in the arts of metal alloy, iron clubfaces began to rise in popularity. At the same time, the harder guttie also demanded that clubs be stronger lest the delicate hickory shafts crack on impact. The new gutta material early on acquired a reputation for

Mesh pattern gutta-percha golf ball mold.

jarring the body of the player at the moment of impact, a touch of violence to the golfer of which the feathery had been utterly incapable.

Gradually players began to notice that nicked gutties, increasingly common as iron clubs gained popularity, flew better than balls with a perfectly smooth surface. Since the imperfections gave the ball some advantage, resourceful players sought to enhance the blemishes. From their experimentation, cross-hatching and other conscious patterns were devised, precursors of the dimpling on golf balls now taken for granted.

It would not be until about 1900 that the Haskell ball, patented by an Ohioan named Coburn Haskell in 1898 and subsequently produced by the B. F. Goodrich Company, began to be used. The wound-rubber-core ball would gradually edge the solid gutta-percha ball out of golf forever.

Oakhurst Links opened during this transition in equipment, straddling two eras in golf history—the original, just beginning to wane, and the modern, not yet dawned.

OF THE OAKHURST PLAYERS, each of whom had a handicap, Lionel Torin was the most experienced, so he doubtless set the playing standard. He was also known to have a bit of a temper. Once in autumn—the year is not known—on a day raw enough to leave the knuckles white but not cold enough to call off the golf game, Torin missed a putt on the ninth green to lose a match. In a volley of self-disgust and derision, he declared, walking off toward Montague's porch, "I expect to play in hell on a green like this!"

Montague, who won this match, exemplifying the wry sporting spirit of play at Oakhurst, let Torin cool off, waited a day, and then sat at his desk in the library and carefully wrote him an original verse to soothe his frustration. It was surely the first golf poem written in America:

> *They play in Hell on a slippery green*
> *With a red-hot iron and a melting cleek;*
> *With a driver on fire and a brimstone ball;*
> *And the putter too hot to hold at all;*
> *And the Devil dormie, with fiendish glee*
> *Says "Play one more round through Eternite."*

Russell Montague's original poem.

We have no record of how many such poetic rounds the Oakhurst group may have played, but according to Montague himself in a 1936 article, "We played continuously for about ten years." Word of the eccentricity going on at Montague's spread through the environs. According to Florence Flynn, occasionally a neighbor, visitor, or guest at the Greenbrier would wander up the road to watch the play, for "they were looked upon by their neighbors and friends as victims of an insane fad or hobby." The first fairway and green stood next to the road, but each of the nine holes was visible from that point. No one who saw them—fine mustachioed men all, dressed in parlor clothes, yet outdoors even in the rainiest weather—had likely ever encountered golf before. So the act of swinging at a small white ball and carrying odd-looking sticks under their arms—golf bags were not yet used—then stopping the game to search through the grass and clover if a ball could not be found, made the Oakhurst players "the subject of great curiosity."

Flynn is also the chronicler of what has become a classic of early Oakhurst lore. According to her article, on an unspecified day the Reverend R. H. Mason, a well-known clergyman from Richmond who often visited the Greenbrier area and knew the Montague family, drove his wagon up to Oakhurst to see firsthand the spectacle he'd been hearing about. He got there just as the retinue was driving the first hole, and in time to hear Montague, who had hit last, cursing the result of his shot: Montague's drive had landed in the ditch just at the curve in the road, virtually at Mason's feet. Mason told Montague he was being needlessly melodramatic over such a tiny mishap. According to Flynn, "Dr. Mason remarked that it was easy, and that any baby could play. Montague handed him his driver and told him to see what he could do."

Mason, who had never held a golf club before, let alone tried to hit a golf ball with one, walked up the road to the first teeing area near Montague's house. What ensued must have been hilariously relived by the group that night around the fireplace, for Mason outright whiffed the ball several times, then managed a weak excuse for contact, just enough to slice his ball in the very same ditch as Montague. Then, Flynn recorded, "after he had played over a hundred strokes, he made the hole." There is no mention of how the other players hid their bemusement. However, when Mason at last walked off the golf course, his dignity and clerical comportment barely intact, he was heard to murmur that the humiliating experience just visited upon him was surely "a science" and not a game.

The Oakhurst members played twelve months of the year, even though the temperature in January in the Greenbrier valley often fell below zero. In fact, to spice their friendship, according to Montague, they competed for a medal. Named the Challenge Medal, the piece was designed and commissioned from the leading gold- and silversmith at the time, Dieges and Clust. Clust was a businessman, and Dieges an ex-soldier who would go on to become an Olympic athlete on the U.S. tug-of-war team. Though how the golfers and this firm found each other is unknown, it is possible that Montague had heard of it, for Dieges and Clust did have an office in Boston, as well as in New York, Pittsburgh, Chicago, Providence, and New Orleans. The firm would eventually win commissions for such heraldic medals as the Congressional Medal of Honor.

The Oakhurst Challenge medal, adorned with a crest

The Oakhurst Challenge Medal.

of green-and-white regal ribbon, was engraved hand-somely with crossed golf clubs, four golf balls, and the words "Far and Sure," the same words carved in the wall in a lane off Edinburgh's Royal Mile to commemorate the legendary late-seventeenth-century match in which Scotland vanquished England. Perhaps Montague had visited the wall in 1875 and saw the words himself, or perhaps his Scottish friends called it forth as the only acceptable motto for their own personal golf course. However it happened, "Far and Sure" became America's first golf logo, and the Challenge Medal the first prize awarded for the competitive playing of golf in the country.

Montague won the Challenge Medal several times, and Roderick MacLeod won it at least once, according to Montague, but it is unknown how often Torin, with his superior skill, gained victory. The group even established a special Christmas tournament, which was played for six

*Back row (left to right): Mew Frazier Montague (Russell's brother),
and Roderick MacLeod. The women are unknown. Front row: Cary
Montague, Russell Montague (with guitar), Margaret Prescott
Montague, and Alexander MacLeod*

successive years and thus would have been the first regular golf tournament played in America.

Oakhurst was so novel that when some guests from the Greenbrier came over one day, apparently just to pay a visit to the Montagues for the sake of meeting some of the local gentry, they were left speechless as they stepped out of the wagon by the golf match under way, the Oakhurst players oblivious to the gallery.

The guests watched for a couple of holes, and one of them commented disdainfully on how obviously well-bred men of reputation were wasting their time. As recorded by Flynn, the scornful observer quipped, "Well, I did play marbles when I was a kid, but by god this is the first time I've seen men play."

THOUGH NO RECORD EXISTS of any communication between the Oakhurst players and the founders of other clubs, a number of them followed on Oakhurst's heels. One of these, the Dorset Field Club in Vermont, was organized in 1886, though some golfers informally hit golf balls in the vicinity earlier than that. The legend on a map depicting the golf course layout states, "The course was planned and laid out on Sunday, September 12, 1886."

In Pennsylvania, Joseph M. Fox, who had experienced golf in Scotland, reportedly laid out some holes on his family estate at Foxburg in 1885. He offered the land to create the Foxburg Country Club, formally organized in 1887 with five holes, enlarged to nine in 1888. In the same year the venerable St. Andrews Club in Tuxedo, New York, was opened and is officially recognized as the oldest continuously operating golf club in America. Continuing the trend, the golf course designer Charles Macdonald built the Chicago Golf Club in 1894, America's

An 1888 golf match at the St. Andrews Club.

first eighteen-hole course, just as the U.S. Golf Association itself was being founded.

Indeed, the period during which Oakhurst was active coincided with a burst of golf popularity that would see almost 1,000 golf courses built in America by 1900—more than in England and Scotland combined. Yet while golf swept the American continent as the twentieth century dawned, Oakhurst Links slipped into slumber, its Scottish protagonists returned home, its fairways growing over.

6

THE FAIRWAYS QUIET

WHEN ASKED IN 1929 how the Oakhurst players came to break up, Russell Montague remarked, "Well, the boys just drifted away." Montague never stipulated a specific date for dissolution, but if, as he said, the group played for ten years or so, the Oakhurst Club would have been disbanded by 1900. It is not known when the last round they played as a group took place, or when the Scotsmen left America.

Given the significance of Oakhurst Links, though, it does seem extraordinary that four of its five main protagonists passed on no record of it to relatives or the golf world back in Scotland and England, kingdom and birthplace of golf. Surely, having built a golf course deep in the American frontier would have made an astounding answer to the question, "How did you spend your time over there?" Yet no letters or diaries remain in their ancestral homes, nor memories in the minds of their descendants. Of course, letters do get lost, and each generation gradually has fewer and fewer custodians of its history. In retrospect, though, it is more likely that the MacLeods, Grant, and Torin returned home completely unaware that their Oakhurst experiment had any meaning at all. By the 1900s golf had been transformed into a craze and was well on its way to becoming a global industry. The Oakhurst experience possibly paled for the once expatriate men of Scotland, now that they were home.

There is no record of how long Lionel Torin's visit to America lasted. He kept at his golf and in 1889 was back in Ceylon, playing in the fall tournament of the Royal Colombo Golf Club. The prizes were gold and silver medals and a cigarette case, none of which he won, even though he shot 49–46 for a gross score of 95, net of 88, given his "allowance," or handicap, of seven. Scores like this would have made him one of the better golfers of the era.

Torin made his way at some point back to England, though he held on to his interests in Ceylon until 1902. According to his great-niece Joanna Myrtle Torin, he was a first-rate yachtsman who spent the summers taking on the fierce winds of Scotland at Bunchrew. There townspeople called him "the old man," a Scottish nickname not unlike "the skipper." Thin but fit, Torin remained handsome in old age. According to the Torin family history, he disparaged a charcoal portrait done of him when he returned from Ceylon, possibly after a bout with malaria, as looking like "the devil dug up." He died in 1928 in London, unmarried and without children.

The MacLeod brothers spent roughly twenty years in Virginia. According to a nephew, they returned to England mainly because their mother, a widow who had a modest fortune, pulled the plug on the expenses of her wanderlust sons.

Alexander MacLeod worked as a land agent back in England, and also acquired a major interest in a cattle business specializing in the rare beef breed known as British Whites. He married a woman named Ella on his return from West Virginia, and he died in 1951 at the age of ninety-three, surviving the last few months, according to his nephew, on nothing but whisky.

Roderick MacLeod, on the other hand, returned to the family homestead at Forres. He lived there with his sister Anna at Dalvey Cottage until his death in 1940, at the age of eighty. Nothing is known of his final years. Whether either of the brothers ever played golf again is unknown, though Norman, their elder brother, may well have kept them active in the game. An avid player, he donated two silver trophy jugs to the Forres Golf Club,

which opened in 1889 next door to the Cluny Hydropathic Institute.

The MacLeod birthplace, Dalvey Cottage, still stands,
and Dalvey proper, considered one of Scotland's great
manor houses, remains a residence for the MacLeod
family. However, the only trace of the brothers' American
sojourn to have survived in MacLeod hands is a box of
stuffed birds behind glass. In this taxidermist's sampler,
each specimen is perched on a twig and neatly labeled—
Baltimore Oriole, Scarlet Tanager, Purple Grackle, and
Cardinal—the blue-black fountain pen ink on the tags
fading but still readable: "White Sulphur Springs, 1895."

George Grant spent most of his time when he returned from West Virginia in London, where he had established an address as of 1901, in Norwood. This
London suburb was then popular with retired civil ser-
vants and military men, which would have put Grant in
familiar social company. He was a member of the Dulwich and Sydenham Golf Club, begun in 1893 by a
handful of stalwarts not unlike Grant's American friends.
The founders of Dulwich and Sydenham had been so enamored of the game that they declared themselves a golf
club, even though the course on which they were playing
had been laid out in secret by a farmer on land he didn't
even own. The golf went on unbeknownst to the absent
landowners for some time, until the club properly in-

corporated itself on land it did own. How well Grant played, and whether he recounted his American adventure to his London friends, will never be known, for most of the club's early records were lost in a fire in World War II when the original clubhouse was struck by a bomb in the blitz.

In fact, when Grant left America, he may have planned one day to return to West Virginia, because he rented his Greycliffe estate for a while rather than selling it. He and Russell Montague had launched a business together in 1884, intending to develop a mineral spring nearby as well as a vein of coal discovered on the same land. There is no further record of this venture, but Grant was prominent enough in the area for a local newspaper, the *Greenbrier Independent*, to note in its pages his return from an 1888 trip to Scotland.

Grant's first tenant, in roughly 1898, was M. E. Ingalls, president of the Chesapeake and Ohio Railroad, and a good choice to appreciate the Greycliffe ambience. Ingalls's son Fay wrote a book titled *The Valley Road*, in which he remarked that his father, "like all who come to these mountains, fell in love with the area."

Fay Ingalls also remembered that a "few English and Scotsmen were living" near what he called "Grant's Farm" when his family rented it. Ingalls also knew Russell Montague and his son Cary. The two boys, close in age, used some of Montague's precious Scottish golf clubs at Oakhurst to "knock a ball about his pasture." Ingalls writes that Russell himself made each of the boys a golf club at "the farm blacksmith shop."

By this point, the C & O Railroad had pushed its tracks deeper into the mountains, up to Hot Springs of Virginia, where the famous hotel Homestead, even older than the Greenbrier, was being refurbished. Fay Ingalls admitted having gotten attracted to golf on the "Montague meadows" and claims to have passed "the bug" on to his father. By 1899 the aura of Oakhurst Links had jumped state lines with the opening of the Virginia Hot Springs Golf and Tennis Club, founded by M. E. Ingalls at the Homestead.

The MacLeods stayed in touch with George Grant, who died peacefully of old age in London in November 1923 at the age of eighty-four. Alexander MacLeod was still sufficiently a friend to be named by Grant as the executor of his will. Grant, a wealthy man at his death, still owned property in Virginia. He left his personal estate to his nephews, never having married or having children of his own. Though he may have left Scotland for America under the cloud of an illicit romance, it seemed, he harbored no animosity toward his living relatives when he returned. In fact, a nephew was present at the time of Grant's death. In a tantalizing bit of historic possibility, the full name of the nephew, the son of George's brother James, was actually Montague James. Perhaps Grant's brother had met Russell Montague before George did, developing a sufficient enough friendship to give his son an uncommon first name.

Grange Manor, in Forres, is still in the Grant Peterkin family, its furnishings largely unchanged since George Grant sailed for America. In a framed montage on the parlor wall, the little boy he once was still runs in a cut black-paper silhouette with his sister and brother, holding a riding crop, and his youthful portrait hangs in its original place on the staircase.

※

RUSSELL MONTAGUE KEPT in touch with his golfing friends for a time. He took special delight in hearing from George Grant about the unlikely, wandering trail of the golf poem he had long before written for Lionel Torin so long ago, what Montague himself called "a bit of doggerel."

After Grant returned to England, he had been playing golf with a new partner, presumably at the Dulwich and Sydenham. Out of the blue, possibly after missing a hellish putt, the stranger quoted a few philosophically poetic lines—the exact words Montague had composed to soothe Torin back in West Virginia after Torin had missed his final putt and lost a match. When Grant, stupefied, asked the man where the poem had come from, the fellow said he had picked it up in India. Thus Montague's lines, composed at Oakhurst, were carried back to Ceylon and India by Torin, who must have quoted them to other frustrated players. Montague was amazed. "Apparently my ribald verse had made its way nearly around the world," he observed in his 1929 interview with Innis Brown, adding wryly, "It struck me as rather a coincidence that a man returning from India should have happened on Grant, one of the five men in the world who knew the origin of the verse."

Though Montague's own land reverted to nature after his friends left, golf proliferated in the vicinity. In 1913 a revamped Greenbrier Hotel opened, with a new eighteen-hole golf course, named the Number One and later the Old White—a classically beautiful layout designed by Charles Blair Macdonald. With this advance, the Greenbrier established an unrivaled beachhead in the world of resort golf, and Montague frequented it as he grew older. There he could be easily spotted in straw hat and knickers, his favorite golf garb. He may also have gotten to know the golf architect Macdonald, for according to the *New York Times* in 1914, the famed course designer was due to visit Oakhurst that year while visiting the Old White, though no record of an Oakhurst visit survives. If

Montague and Macdonald did meet, surely Montague would have been the source of the reference to Oakhurst in Macdonald's book *Scotland's Gift.*

Harriet Montague, Russell's wife, died in 1919. Russell and his children, Cary and Margaret, continued to live on and off at Oakhurst, mainly in summer, dividing their time between Richmond, Virginia, and Greenbrier County. The overgrown golf course played practically no role in their lives.

Cary and Margaret Montague had been very close as children, Cary being the older by fifteen months. According to the memoir of Cary's granddaughter, Harriet, both Cary and Margaret had been diagnosed with retinitis pigmentosa at a young age, and the doctor had expected they would be completely blind by the time they were in their mid-twenties. While this never happened, both wore thick glasses and hearing aids all their lives.

Cary Montague had been impressed into ecclesiastical service at the tender age of seventeen, in roughly 1894, by a local reverend, George Easter. Easter had to make an arduous forty-mile wagon and train trip from his home church to minister to the local faithful, but only had the stamina to cover the distance every fifth Sunday. Easter asked Cary to take over, since he appeared to be a devout boy. Cary agreed, and though he drew only four church-goers on his first Sunday of preaching, he kept at it. He then became an elementary school teacher, also acquiring sufficient public stature to run for the position of justice of the peace. He lost the election, but found he loved politics.

In fact, during Cary's losing campaign in 1900, William McKinley was running for president, with Theodore Roosevelt as his running mate. West Virginia had been thick with campaigners and promoters, one of whom was a relative of Roosevelt's. Knowing of Roosevelt's love of the wild, Cary Montague told the fellow that if the Republican slate won, he would send Roosevelt a bear cub straight from the West Virginia mountains.

Montague did just that, for he knew of a family living above Oakhurst who had been raising a black bear cub they wanted to be rid of. Cary bought the bear and tied a tag around its neck that read, "From the Republicans of Greenbrier County, West Virginia, to Theodore Roosevelt, Vice-President of the United States, Oyster Bay, New York."

How Montague shipped the bear to Roosevelt's personal residence is not recorded. However, two years after the shipment, Cary Montague found himself in Washington, D.C., on church business. He decided the bear incident gave him a good excuse to call on President Roosevelt, who had acceded to the office after McKinley's assassination in 1901. The White House was then accessible, and Montague strode straight up to the gatehouse and resolutely asked to see Roosevelt. Rebuffed but undeterred, Montague somehow slipped the guard and made his way inside to a secretary, who admitted Montague to an anteroom where he waited patiently among those who had bona fide appointments with the president. These included men of state from Africa who had come to consult about the Boer War, which had grown into a full-blown conflict.

Cary Montague's turn did eventually come, and the president enthusiastically shook his hand and told Montague that not only had he received the bear some years before, but he had kept it as long as he could as a pet for his own children. When the bear became too large, Roosevelt had sent it to the Central Park Zoo in New York City, thereby, according to Cary's daughter's version, inspiring the creation of the "Teddy" bear.

WHILE CARY MONTAGUE immersed himself in theology and civic life, his sister, Margaret Prescott Montague, pursued a writing career, most of her work inspired by living at Oakhurst. Her vision and hearing being weak, she relied on her memory of sights and sounds of the landscape and filled her books with mountainfolk characters, such as the dashing woodsman Tony Beaver. By 1923 she had published five full-length novels and many short stories under her given name, as well as other books and articles dealing with metaphysical subjects under the pen name "Jane Steger." Her essay "Twenty Minutes of Reality" recounts an out-of-body state of consciousness and was included in a social ethics syllabus at Harvard University.

Margaret also wrote about political events, and in 1919 she won the prestigious O. Henry Award for her short story "England to America." President Woodrow Wilson described it as "the greatest piece of literature" to come out of World War I.

In 1920 Montague's book *Uncle Sam of Freedom Ridge,* a plea in support of U.S. entry to the League of Nations, was made into a hit movie. President Wilson was so moved by the film that he allowed the producers to quote his effusive praise: the film, he said, "breathes of a patriotism so pure and wholesome as to make the other things of life seem of little consequence." On the day the film premiered in White Sulphur Springs, Margaret treated the entire town to tickets.

Still, in those days magazines like the *Atlantic Monthly* paid $40 each for stories, and one of Margaret Montague's earliest book royalty checks in 1906 had been for $13.88. In 1921 Montague found herself trying to buy some of her copyrights back; her publisher was getting ready to put her books out of print. So, renown aside,

Margaret never knew a day of wealth. In fact, even as she tried to keep writing, she and her father took in boarders at Oakhurst for a time, well after Oakhurst Links had ceased to exist.

In opposition to the contrarian liberal leanings of his daughter, Russell Montague was by every account an unflagging conservative with little sympathy for government. He frequently dispensed his opinions in letters to the editor, once calling for the impeachment of Franklin Roosevelt in the *Richmond Times-Dispatch*. He accused the president of "indiscriminate and demagogic attacks on business," and of "promoting class hatred and attempting to build his Utopia on hate instead of good will."

Russell was able to make a modest success of what he came to call Oakhurst Orchards. In fact, there was a big harvest every fall at his apple and peach orchards up above the farmhouse, near where the MacLeod brothers had lived. Ever the amateur professional, Russell had become a true student of soil science. In a meticulous journal, he recorded characteristics of his land, including acidity, alkalinity, and the reasons he planted each crop. He studied the many different types of soils and grasses, and experimented with various methods of irrigation and drainage. He set terra-cotta pipes down in the ground to divert snowmelt to his ponds, keeping

The Oakhurst clubhouse in the 1920s.

them full in summer and preventing the fields from flooding.

All of these activities Russell summed up in a letter to the Harvard alumni in 1912 as the "gentle courtesy of agriculture." He had little new to report to Harvard in his letter of 1924, the last he would send, and he never mentioned a word in any of his correspondence with Harvard about the golf course he had once tended just as carefully.

Montague himself seems not to have realized that his golf course had been any kind of landmark until 1929, when he met Innis Brown, a well-known golf writer at the time who had somehow gotten wind of the Oakhurst story. Brown came to Oakhurst to interview Montague and convinced him that no golf had been played on an organized golf course in America prior to Oakhurst's 1884 debut. As Montague himself put it later, in 1936, when Forrest Jackson came to call for *Rail* magazine: "I formerly called the course laid out on my property at Oakhurst, a very early golf course. I said 'a very early golf course' because although I had seen it stated in several New York papers that it was the first course in America, as I distrust superlatives, I was doubtful about it until the Editor of the American Golfer called on me in 1929 and said that he had made a study of early golf courses and was convinced that this was the first such course in America." Montague had even put up some argument to Brown: "I reminded him that there was a golf course in Georgia much earlier, some time in the Eighteenth Century and he told me he knew all about this club; that they never laid out any links and never played golf, though probably they intended to do so. They contented themselves with a banquet once a year. In fact you might say that the only hole they had was the nineteenth. Remember, this was Georgia before the days of Prohibition and I understand that par for the course was a magnum of champagne."

*Russell Montague (center) playing golf at age ninety-two,
shortly before his death.*

The Oakhurst motto had been "Far and Sure," but
Montague readily admitted that none of the players had
ever been either far or sure in their golf shots. He told
Jackson it was "an excellent motto, but not appropriate
for us as none of us were very 'sure' and we certainly did
not drive very 'far' as we only had the old gutty ball,
which does not carry as the modern ball does." Montague
continued, "As there were only five of us naturally the
links were very rough, but they were very sporting and we
all became very expert with mashies and niblicks, so

much so that when I played later . . . and found myself in a bunker, I thought I had a pretty good lie."

Russell Montague, the man who had been told he would die young, in fact died peacefully in 1945, in his sleep, without apparent suffering, at the age of ninety-three at Margaret's home in Richmond. He had continued playing golf until a few months before his death, his life seeming to well advertise the golf great Bobby Jones's words: "The first purpose of any golf course should be to give pleasure."

For Montague's children, the land tottered between cherished legacy and emotional burden. In 1945 Margaret wrote a friend, "My brother Cary and I were left Oakhurst—share and share alike. I do not know exactly what will happen to it. I rather want to keep it, he rather wants to sell it, and as yet we do not know what we will do about it."

7

THE ERA OF OAKHURST FARM

WHEN RUSSELL MONTAGUE DIED in 1945, Lewis Keller was an up-and-coming entrepreneur learning the ropes of the shipping business, after attending Duke University on a football scholarship. However, his true sporting passion was reserved for golf, and he had been good enough at it to have made a local reputation for himself by the time he was ten in the Virginia Tidewater.

Keller's father, Ross, loved the game and played in a regular Saturday foursome, which his son had begged to join before he was barely old enough to attend elementary school. At age eight, in 1931, Lewis received his first club—a Walter Beckett mid-iron. His father had unwrapped and measured the club, cut it down to a perfect height for Lewis to swing, rewhipped it with black cord, and regripped it with leather from one of his old clubs. So Lewis could practice, his father stretched a paint tarpaulin tight across the garage door. Soon all the neighbors around the Keller house knew when Lewis was working on his golf game by the constant thump as the boy fired ball after ball, hour after hour, into the canvas.

After a few months, when Lewis was making contact with the ball consistently, the garage tarp was no longer challenge enough. Instead of just the feedback of sound, Lewis was ready for the feedback of space. He cast his eye on the vacant lot across the street. Dutifully, he first got permission from the owner of the lot, Clarence Ball. Ball too was a golfer, and his daughter Nancy would marry Tom Strange, a golf professional. They would have twin sons, one of whom, Curtis, would grow up to have his name climb the leader boards of the world's major golf tournaments.

Lewis took his father's lawn mower to the lot and began shaping his fairways. Then he walked back and forth, pacing off an eight-year-old's version of a three-hole layout. He took his mother's gardening trowel, dug out three cups, and placed twigs in the holes as flagsticks. In time Ross cut down a few more irons, a putter, and a driver for his son, and roughly a year after acquiring his first cutdown mid-iron, Lewis played golf well enough to earn a slot in the weekly family foursome.

At the age of ten, Lewis Keller played in his first golf tournament. He did not win that day, but his respectable showing did make the local paper. By high school, Lewis

Lewis Keller (far right) on the golf team of Maury High School,
Virginia Beach, Virginia.

was captain of the school golf team, and in his senior year, 1942, Keller and a friend hitched a ride to the Princess Anne Country Club in Virginia Beach, Virginia, to watch a professional tournament. Then, the golf circuit was a makeshift affair with meager galleries and barely enough prize money to keep the winners in golf balls. Eager golf enthusiasts could easily get up close to the legends, and Keller had come to see the current pride of Virginia, the twenty-nine-year-old Sam Snead.

Snead, already a sensation with his long drives and effortless swing, was giving an exhibition, and Keller threaded his way through the crowd to a prime vantage point. The two did not meet that day, though twelve years later their friendship would flourish, leading directly to the rebirth of Oakhurst.

After Duke and a stint in the navy, Lewis Keller entered the shipping industry and discovered a passion for work and business to rival his love of golf. He moved to New York City in 1949 and soon was introduced to the Winged Foot Golf Club and its two famous courses, designed by A. W. Tillinghast. Joining the club, Keller signed up for lessons with the club's renowned professional, Claude Harmon, the father of Tiger Woods's coach, Butch Harmon. Under Claude Harmon's guidance, the self-taught Keller honed a scratch game and began receiving invitations to and playing in leading amateur tournaments, including the Crump, Valentine, National Amateur, and Crosby, and a highlight of the amateur circuit, the Spring Festival at the Greenbrier resort in White Sulphur Springs, an invitation-only event that brought together about two hundred amateurs and fifty professionals. Still, though Oakhurst is only three miles from the Greenbrier, in all his early visits Keller never heard of Montague's golf course.

Lewis Keller married Rosalie Jenkins in October 1950. Their courtship had taken place as much on a golf course as off, even though she had not a shred of interest in playing herself. Keller's entrepreneurial instincts led him away from the shipping business, and he purchased a one-third interest in a lumber company and pursued other projects. He and Rosalie had two sons, Lewis Jr. and John, by the summer of 1954. By then too, the fast-paced pressures of business life had given Keller a stomach ulcer, and his physician ordered an immediate vacation and break. For Lewis Keller, any rest period had to include golf, so the Kellers headed for the Greenbrier, which had become a favorite since Keller's first Spring Festival.

Sam Snead, then forty-one, was the resident club professional at the resort, which had become a golfing mecca. Snead was well known for the pleasure he took in winning bets from top amateurs who jumped at the chance to play with him when they came to the hotel. After watching Keller's skilled practice, Snead decided Keller might be a hot new target and sent one of his assistants to ask Lewis if he would like to play a game the next day. Keller, unsurprisingly, committed every shot of that round to memory.

> The two of us played the Old White, my favorite course. Sam gave me two shots a side, and we also played a medal bet. After a few days, I was up $250, and Sam and I were joking as we started what would be our last match for that visit because I was returning to New York the following day. Sam made sure I knew he intended to get his money back. I told him that if he didn't win it back that day, I would take him back to New York, and we would just finish the match at Winged Foot. So we played the front nine, and I won. At the turn Sam said, "Okay, Lewis, let's make it double or nothing." I was still just playing super, and so was Sam. I had been shooting 70 or 71 every day and, with the four strokes I was getting, he would

have had to shoot 66 or 67 to beat me. We got to the 12th hole, which is a long par 5. I teed up and hit a beautiful drive, right down the middle. Then Sam hit an amazing drive that landed on the fairway right near a landmark for Sam—a slight mound, from where he knew he could hit a one iron to the green. I was behind him, and so I hit my second shot right in front of the green. From there, I knew I could chip it up and get a 4 for birdie—since I was getting a stroke on the hole.

Sam walked over, looked me in the eye, and said "I'm gonna get you right here. I'm gonna nail this one iron." And he did. The ball landed about three feet from the pin, and he was right. That shook me. I chipped it short and missed my putt, and I made a 5. He made eagle three, and he beat me and won the back nine. So we were dead even. It was just a wonderful game. We shook hands and walked in together.

Keller left the next morning, but he enjoyed many more rounds with Snead as time went on. Keller soon became a regular at the Greenbrier Spring Festival. He teed off and mingled with many public figures, including Bing Crosby, the duke and duchess of Windsor, Ben Hogan, Gene Sarazen, and of course Snead, who was becoming a true friend. In 1955 Lewis was paired with Gary Player, and they came in second. The amateur golf circuit became the backbone of Keller's life.

Rosalie Keller never did acquire a taste for playing golf

herself, but she absorbed golf knowledge like a sponge. By the time she and Lewis had been married a few years, she could distinguish an upright, flat, inside, or outside swing, which players pronated, and who had an enviable follow-through. Meanwhile, too, the Kellers developed many golf-based friendships, among them Gardner Dickinson, who was a well-known pro at the time, and his wife, Della.

Increasingly the Kellers were drawn to the Greenbrier landscape, which would, as it had for Montague and his friends, become a defining element in their lives. In 1959 they decided to find a summer home in the area. Hearing of their search, though never imagining the implications of what he was about to suggest, Snead proposed that the Kellers take a ride up Big Draft Road and look at a place called Oakhurst. Not only might it possibly be for sale, Snead drawled, there was another tantalizing detail: In addition to the farmhouse, which would need some work, and about a hundred acres with a beautiful view, an old golf course had once existed on the land.

Snead paused, Keller remembers, and looked at Lewis to see if the words had stuck. "A golf course?" Lewis echoed. Snead nodded. He told Keller he had been up there himself in 1938 to hit some balls, when he could still make out some of the holes. The Greenbrier had been hosting the first White Sulphur Springs Open, and Snead was a featured contender. However, it was a side event that had taken Snead to Oakhurst. Fraser Coron,

Sam Snead at the overgrown Oakhurst Links in 1938.

Montague's club maker, was then eighty-four years old and still making golf clubs. In between rounds of the Open, Coron was being feted as "America's first club maker" and giving demonstrations of his venerable skills. Snead, who had gotten his own start in golf by repairing clubs, visited Coron's workshop, and when asked to hit a few balls up at the old Oakhurst golf course, Snead was more than happy to oblige.

Snead had not been back to Oakhurst since, he told Keller, but he reckoned the original golf course was by then nothing but brush, wildflowers, and weeds. Snead arranged for his assistant to give the Kellers a lift up to Oakhurst, since they hadn't ever driven the narrow back roads and blind curves near the Greenbrier.

[115]

Sam Snead and Fraser Coron at Coron's workshop, 1938.

After taking the right turn off Big Draft Road up an even narrower road called Montague Drive, the Kellers crossed a small wooden bridge over Dry Creek and then spotted the sprawling white farmhouse up ahead. At the entrance to the property, a tattered white sign hung:

OAKHURST LINKS—

SITE OF THE FIRST ORGANIZED GOLF CLUB IN AMERICA

Established 1884

Owner—Russell W. Montague

[116]

When they stepped out of the car and looked over the open fields and beyond, they could see precious little golf course. From where they were standing on the front lawn, they could barely discern the layout's outline, now just a shadow on the land, a fairway line or raised mound here and there, all the slopes now plush with grass and the passage of time. Instead, the Kellers remember most being awed by the beauty of the place.

They turned at the sound of a voice as Cary Montague, leaning on his cane, walked out of the house and greeted them. Margaret Montague had died in 1955, and her brother, now eighty-two, was stooped and frail. Still, the Kellers remember, his blue eyes were warm and alert, even through the thick eyeglasses he wore, and he had a firm handshake and full smile.

With his sister's death, Cary Montague was intent on selling Oakhurst because he simply couldn't afford to keep it up. He had been slow to warm to prospective buyers, nevertheless; God-fearing and modest, he worried that speculators might buy Oakhurst and convert it into a casino. The economy of Greenbrier County was still weak, with plenty of rural poverty, and gambling was rumored to be the Greenbrier region's next economic boom business.

The elderly minister showed Lewis and Rosalie through the house, which was actually two separate buildings joined by an upstairs walkthrough. The main house consisted of a large book-filled library, which had been used as a schoolroom in earlier years, and a dining room, living room, and small den, which had been the original Oakhurst Links club room. Here and there were scattered golf memorabilia from the original Montague era, including a framed ensemble of portraits of the founders.

The Kellers toured the warren of rooms upstairs, each with shallow charcoal-burning fireplaces and pans to catch the ashes, still sitting where they'd been placed in the nineteenth century. A glinting chandelier hung in the entrance hall. Rosalie Keller noticed that the slant of sunlight through the glass transom above the front door had thrown a rainbow on the chandelier, even through the layers of dust. Nobody had lived at Oakhurst full-time for years.

Rosalie Keller left her husband to talk in private with Cary Montague and walked up toward the woods to take some photographs. She remembers sensing then that she and Lewis would buy the property, and as she walked back down the slope, she saw her husband and Cary shaking hands, and heard Lewis assuring Montague that gambling would never come to pass at Oakhurst.

❧

LEWIS KELLER HAD BEEN intrigued by the idea of owning a property critical to the history of golf, but neither he nor Rosalie intended to bring the course back to life at the time they bought Oakhurst. Nonetheless, they did become immediate and dedicated stewards of the Oakhurst memorabilia that Cary Montague had passed along so it would stay with the house. This included the original Oakhurst Challenge Medal, which the Kellers put in a vault for safekeeping. Cary Montague had also given them a replica medal the Montague family had had struck, and the Kellers placed it under a dome of glass displayed on a table in the hall. They kept the framed portrait of the founders of Oakhurst Links—Russell, George, Alexander, Roderick, and Lionel—in its prominent place over the main hall table.

Lewis Keller even followed up a suggestion by Cary Montague's wife, Margretta, to gather more information about the course from an elderly local man who had worked at Oakhurst during the golfing period. The man remembered some unusual details, such as that the Oakhurst players used a ball called the Eclipse—which Charles Macdonald noted in his book had been popular in 1886—that they cost thirty-five cents each, and that each player carried only one ball as he played. Keller also learned that occasionally the Oakhurst club members paid local boys, twenty-five cents a round to caddy.

Still, Oakhurst was to be the Kellers' summer retreat, and the golfing history of the land took a backseat to another vision that had begun to form in Lew Keller's mind. His entrepreneurial instincts led him to imagine that the property could achieve at least some degree of self-sustenance. Gradually, Keller began to consider turning Oakhurst into a horse farm.

Keller had always been mesmerized by thoroughbred racehorses. As a boy, he had been riveted by the newsreel of the widely publicized 1938 race between Seabiscuit and War Admiral, the two horses pounding down the stretch until Seabiscuit pulled away to win in the last quarter mile. He had also recently read a *New York Times* article on the thoroughbred breeding business, and its potential for profit, albeit risky, appealed to him.

Keller's venture into the business of horses was self-taught at every stage. He knew on sight that Oakhurst's slopes were covered with bluegrass, and he reasoned intuitively that the heavy snowmelt in West Virginia would leave behind ample nitrogen in the soil. He believed the slopes of Oakhurst would be as ideal for galloping and grazing horses as for a golf course layout. The overgrown fields lying down the slope from the house, where most of the golf course had been, were cleared of brush and reseeded.

Keller also built stables in what had once been the exact middle of the course, and white board fences crisscrossed the old fairways, dividing the fields into different sizes of paddocks. The horses soon followed, and by 1963 Oakhurst Farm, as Keller had renamed the property, was a going concern.

※

WHILE LEWIS KELLER had transformed his land, vestiges of the old golf course remained, and in August 1963 one of them surfaced. Keller enlisted his sons to work on the farm, and one of their primary tasks was to clear rocks and other objects from the fields, which could only be done by hand. A thoroughbred that stepped on a sharp rock or tripped on a hidden root could well be made lame forever. Every spring, like perennial budding flowers, a new crop of rocks appeared in the fields and had to be picked out by hand. It would take five summers of picking out rocks, and painstakingly building up the topsoil, before there was dirt enough to stop the rocks from appearing every year.

Ten-year-old John had developed a fascination with fossils and other artifacts from the past, and the rock clearing became an opportunity for him to expand his collection, which included several Indian arrowheads and two Civil War musket balls, one Union and one Confederate. That August morning, John Keller walked down to what the Kellers referred to as the bottom field—the bot-

*The gutta-percha balls found by Mark Waid and
John Keller at Oakhurst.*

tom of the property near Dry Creek. After several hours
of clearing rocks, he was preparing for lunch when his eye
was drawn to an object that he first thought was a walnut.
He dug it out of the dirt and held it up to the sun to study
it carefully. It was caked with dirt, though he could see it
was perfectly round, and John knew it could not be natural. He almost threw it away but hesitated and put it in
his pocket instead.

That evening John showed the object to his father,
who recognized it immediately as an old golf ball. What
John had found would prove to be a museum-quality ar-
tifact—a gutta-percha ball used by the original Oakhurst
players, dating from the mid-1800s. Lewis Keller knew
the importance of the find, and kept the ball in his top
dresser drawer for the next thirty years.

John Keller's discovery aside, it was Lewis Jr. who was

most in tune with the lingering aura of Oakhurst Links. Like his father, he had developed an early passion for the game, and he too received the gift of a cut-down golf club from his father. When golf friends of his parents came over from the Greenbrier, Lewis Jr. joined them on the Oakhurst porch. While virtually no golfer in America at that time had ever heard of Oakhurst Links, by the time he was fourteen Lewis Jr. had memorized its history. From the Oakhurst porch, he could see the golf course under what in Oakhurst Farm parlance was known as the bottom, middle, and upper fields.

In 1965, there were still elevations and depressions in the land reminiscent of a golf course, especially a triangular area formed by what was probably the first green, second tee, and eighth green. As it happened, the horse fence lines didn't interfere with those three holes of the course. I would take my club and go down there by myself in the afternoons and play golf, and it was my own private course, and I would imagine playing tournaments against Ben Hogan or Sam Snead, and play those three holes over and over in different sequence. I learned a lot from doing that. There were no tee boxes and no cups left on the land. In reality, I was simply knocking a golf ball with a seven iron out in a horse pasture. But in my imagination I had a match to play.

My first shot had to carry a small creek, which was actually there, but in my mind's eye it was full of water, not rocks. I had to understand what that creek meant in my game. After a lot of practice, I learned how to manufacture different shots. Off the tee I had to hook it around a big oak tree, then there was the hill, and I knew the ball would roll down to the left so I had to plan for that. Playing around and through these natural occurrences helped me judge distances and improved my accuracy.

Lewis Keller took any chance he could to play with his son, as horses grazed and galloped around them. On one occasion they were hitting balls up to an imaginary flagstick on what they called simply "the green," one of the slightly raised areas they assumed had been a putting area, since it looked like it had once been deliberately flattened out. As they bent over in the high grass to retrieve their golf balls, they spotted a clear circle in the ground, and knew instantly it was one of the original Oakhurst Links cups. The two plunged their fingers into the ground and tried to pull it out, but the old rusted metal crumbled in their hands. Their find, however, would prove to be invaluable twenty-five years later as a guide to the original layout of Oakhurst Links.

❧

BY THE MID-1970s the breeding program at Oakhurst Farm was gaining a reputation, and Keller set his sights

A brood mare and foal on what was the ninth green area.

on having his yearlings accepted into the sale at Keeneland, Kentucky, the most prestigious horse auction in the country.

Keller hired a young local man, John Fury, who was known for his gentle way with horses, to be in charge of the yearling barn. Fury, it turned out, had a special touch. He groomed the yearlings meticulously and spent days teaching the horses how to stand squarely, not to paw the ground, jerk their heads at the pressure of the lead shank, nor mischievously nip the trainer's hand—behavior that could reduce a yearling's appeal.

Fury's hard work paid off. Not only were Oakhurst

yearlings accepted into the Keeneland sale, they brought respectable prices and an infusion of pride for Oakhurst Farm. Over the next fifteen years, Oakhurst strengthened its reputation as a small but quality operation. The Kellers even kept a few horses off the market to race themselves, their jockeys wearing shimmering green-and-white silks with a logo the Kellers designed of crossed golf clubs, inspired by the original Oakhurst "Far and Sure" logo.

All the while Keller operated Oakhurst Farm, he kept in close touch with his golf circuit and friends. In 1992 he entered the golf course business, starting a project in northern West Virginia with Lewis Keller Jr., then forty-one, and Gardner Dickinson, Keller's longtime golfing friend.

The West Virginia project attracted the interest of the noted golf course designer Bob Cupp, who knew Dickinson but hadn't yet met Keller. To discuss the business of the deal, Keller invited all the parties to meet at Oakhurst. During the evening, in full view of the seven mountain ranges, unchanged from the day Montague first beheld them, Cupp, himself a golf history buff who had heard snippets of the Oakhurst tale from Dickinson, asked Keller to flesh out the story.

As Keller remembers, the two were leaning on the fence that kept the horses from coming up on the front lawn, looking at the grazing broodmares and foals. Keller told Cupp that the horses were probably standing on what had once been the ninth green, since it was the flat

Gardner Dickinson, Bob Cupp, and Lewis Keller the evening they
first discussed restoring Oakhurst.

area nearest to the house. Keller continued pointing out the juxtapositions before their eyes—here was a green, perhaps; there, a possible tee.

Cupp, his curiosity mounting, asked if there was any written documentation, and Keller promptly produced not only Russell Montague's original handwritten irrigation journal—the equivalent of a minor textbook for a landscape architect—but also the replica of the Oakhurst Challenge Medal and the original gutta-percha ball found by John Keller when he was pitching rocks. What golf lover could resist an errant shot from the nineteenth century? By the end of the evening, Cupp had asked Keller if he had ever considered restoring the course, for here was a chance to bring an ancient game and its ways back to life.

❧

CUPP RETURNED HOME to Atlanta and tried the idea on his friend, the acclaimed golf writer Dick Taylor. Intrigued with what Cupp told him, Taylor was puzzled as to why almost no one had heard that Oakhurst was the first golf course in America. He visited and grilled Keller on the historic facts, and it was only then, when the idea of restoration had emerged, that Lewis Keller realized the tragic magnitude of an event that had occurred just after he and Rosalie had bought Oakhurst from Cary Montague.

In early 1960 Cary's wife, Margretta, had invited the Kellers to her Richmond home to pick up some additional artifacts from the Oakhurst Links period that were stored in their garage, including original golf clubs from the Montague era and a cache of unspecified papers. The night before the Kellers planned to drive to Richmond, an electrical fire had swept through the Montague garage, burning it to the ground. The record of a decade of historic play at Oakhurst was reduced to what had been left in the house at Oakhurst.

Amazingly, Margaret Montague, the prolific writer who was a young girl during the peak of Oakhurst Links play, even caddying for her father now and then, according to her brother, apparently never wrote about the golf course. Not a single word about it exists in the thirteen boxes of her archive at the University of West Virginia in Morgantown, a vast collection of correspondence, drafts, journals, and other writerly evidence of her life at Oakhurst. And though in 1949 it had been Margaret who had instigated a local fund-raising effort to have a plaque placed in the Oakhurst church to honor the beautiful woodcarving work of Fraser Coron, no mention was made at the time of his also working on golf clubs.

Taylor began delving into golf libraries, while Keller himself began to search out more references. Gradually, they built up a historical record, unearthing early articles about Oakhurst, consulting also with the historian of the Greenbrier, Robert Conte. Ultimately, they and the Kellers pulled together everything they could find that had been written about the course, including the *New York Times* piece and the later articles by Innis Brown and Forrest Jackson in which Montague himself is quoted. (Florence Flynn's invaluable 1913 piece for *Golf* did not surface until 1997, when it was sent to Conte from a friend who had uncovered it in the library of the U.S. Golf Association.)

[129]

The research further fueled the enthusiasm Taylor, Cupp, and Keller were building for restoring the course. Still, despite the significant history, Keller was torn. He loved the horse farm as much as he loved golf, and he had to give up one to have the other. Rosalie and Lewis felt they needed some time to think through the options. "We had to get away from Oakhurst to give the idea of bringing back the golf course time to settle," Keller remembers. A filly that had been raised at Oakhurst was running at the Meadowlands, in New Jersey, and Lewis and Rosalie decided to head north for the weekend to take in the race. They had always loved the thrill of watching one of their horses run.

The Kellers found a place on the rail from which to view the post parade. As they watched their horse being led to the track, the green-and-white Oakhurst silks crystallized Keller's thinking. He realized he was one of very few people in the world who knew the significance of the two crossed clubs on the jockey's shirt and the history they represented. The filly prancing in front of him embodied the success of Oakhurst Farm, and Keller understood then that there was nothing more he wanted to achieve there.

Soon after, a perfect stranger drove up the Oakhurst driveway and knocked on the kitchen door. Jim Sloan told Keller that he was interested in going into the thor-

Oakhurst Farm's Tywydd's Tish in the winner's circle.

oughbred business. Sloan was staying at the Greenbrier and had been told by the bartender, the grandson of the caretakers who had worked at Oakhurst for many years, to visit Oakhurst if he was interested in seeing a beautiful horse farm.

Keller took Sloan on a tour of the pastures, and soon the two were immersed in talking about Oakhurst's bloodlines. On their return to the house Sloan made an offer to buy Oakhurst's entire stock of horses, just as Keller himself had immediately purchased Oakhurst from Cary Montague. Keller was stunned, but after consulting with his wife and children, he consummated the deal that afternoon.

A few days later Keller sadly watched his horses leave, then quickly telephoned Bob Cupp. Within a week Cupp was back at Oakhurst, and the two began making a plan to bring the golf course beneath the pastures back to life.

8

PRESENT AT THE CREATION

"IT WILL BE A LOT OF FUN when we walk the course. The course will actually 'happen' at that time," Bob Cupp wrote Lewis Keller just before taking on the Oakhurst project. In April 1994, over just eight days, they found the golf course by feeling it out with their feet and eyes.

The key to rediscovering the layout and scale was to imagine how far a golf ball could have been hit by a player of the Montague era. Cupp's research found that one of the greatest hickory shots ever recorded flew 240 yards in April 1914, hit by a professional named Duncan, playing against the champion, Harry Vardon, at the Sandy Lodge golf course in England. His clubhead, however, would have been larger than the Montague-era needlenose type. Two hundred and forty yards with a needlenose driver, its clubface no wider than two fingers, striking a gutta-percha ball would have been impossible for a group of amateurs like Montague and company.

Keller tracked down a dealer in replica period clubs, and he and Cupp, both well-above-average players, set about hitting shots with tools akin to those in the hands of the Oakhurst founders. As Cupp wrote in his notes, "It was a matter of the golf course following the equipment . . . what we have learned from the gutta percha balls we have hit on the various holes is invaluable. The ballistics are such that 170 yards seems to be a maximum for this site."

There was no doubt where the first hole had been, even though no original drawing of Oakhurst Links had survived. On Lewis Keller's initial visit to Oakhurst in 1959, Cary Montague, virtually blind by then, had taken Keller by the wrist and led him off the porch to point out the first fairway. The pond that had made for a daunting opening hazard was still there, naturally fed by mountain springs, though the grass in the fairway, which had been the pony field during most of the Oakhurst Farm days, had grown to about eight inches.

Apart from proximity to the house, it was easy for Keller and Cupp to see why Montague and company would have chosen this spot for the opening shots of the game. It offered challenge and length, a devilish carry over the pond in an attempt to also carry the slope. Indeed, Innis Brown, in his 1929 article, described number one as a "hard one-shotter, with the old clubs and the mulish old guttie ball. So Mr. Montague had assured me." This meant that for the original Oakhurst designers, the first tee shot was supposed to reach the green—a tall order in any era.

Sure enough, at just about 170 yards down the pony field and across the road, there were pronounced areas of coloration. Cupp sensed this had to have been a green, where perhaps different, more "puttable" grasses had been planted and kept to a different length over time. Looking back up the slope reinforced the green's location: if a player's first shot happened to land on the ridge instead, the setup presented an equally tricky second shot down onto the green, since there was little room between it and the creek.

As a concession, Cupp would slightly enlarge what he saw as the green area, though in the end the average size of Oakhurst greens, at three thousand square feet, was far smaller than the roughly seven thousand square feet of the average modern course. Cupp felt the first Oakhurst green "should be large because it goes away from the shot." It also made an appealing entry to the course.

Cupp and Keller were sure they had recaptured the original outline of number one. However, finding number two was not as easy. They knew at least the general vicinity of the next tee box, because according to golf's

Bob Cupp and Lewis Keller preparing to stake the holes for restoration.

earliest rules, teeing ground and putting green had to be as near to each other as possible. One very early rule reference in 1775 stated, "You must tee your Ball not nearer the hole than two club lengths, nor further distant than four." This admonition made the putting area and the next teeing area virtually one and the same.

Still, from what was likely to be the second tee area, the second fairway was not self-evident. At first glance, it seemed a drive could be directed either of two ways—straight down the line of Dry Creek along what had been the bottom horse field, or angled up to the right across the middle field, somewhat parallel to number one.

Several indentations from what could well have been bunkers caught their eyes, and Keller and Cupp tested the rightward premise to see what a drive to the right would yield. Cupp wrote of the bunkers, "They define the shot to the correct landing area perfectly, and also look nice on the entry. Our shots came down about 150 to 160 yards [uphill] and two big blows might get the player home in two." There was also an alternative, as Cupp noted, for a player who chose to avoid the hill bunkers: the side of the fairway nearest "the creek left of the second leg and the green may prove to be the better part of valor."

Furthermore, since number one tumbled down toward its green, number two could logically have been the perfect reverse, steps of contours leading up and running under the ridgeline of one so as not to waste any land. Cupp focused on finding the actual bunkers on number two, looking for traces of sand. There is no record of where Montague and friends would have gotten sand for their bunkers, and it would certainly not have been the white granular used today. Cupp noted that "this work will not be shaping as we know it, but more of an archaeological dig. The bunkers must be painstakingly edged until the original outline is found."

Given the distance involved in the two "big blows," Cupp and Keller reasoned that number two had to be the 1884 version of a par-five hole. The logical green area just beyond another apparent bunker on the right slope in the second landing zone seemed very small, suggesting that number two had been a challenge.

The clue to the third hole was the "pigtrail" up the slope to the right of the second green. A pigtrail, as Cupp described it, is "a narrow walking path either worn into the soil or graded by hand. It allows players to traverse a slope without falling down or twisting an ankle. . . . an excellent original one has survived."

When Keller and Cupp reached the rise at the top of the little trail, just off the north end of the Montague farmhouse, the direction of the next hole seemed obvious. Far off in the distance, hanging on the farthest slope of the property, was a decidedly flat area that the Kellers had always noticed but never studied. Pronounced and a lightish green like blotting paper, it could certainly have been a putting area. It would also have been a dangerous place for a green, since beyond it was a steep drop-off and uninterrupted forest, likely the natural outer boundary of the original Oakhurst Links.

If this had indeed been a green, it was likely to have been number four rather than three, for the distance from the top of the pigtrail, some four hundred yards, would have been impossible within the concept of par at the time. More than likely, Keller and Cupp reasoned, the distant green was a full hole away, and number three was situated somewhere in between, short enough to fit, but long enough to get the player in position for number four. Also, after the long play of numbers one and two, the Oakhurst players could well have sought some variety in the form of a shorter hole and a different mix of shots, calling more for precision than distance. They also could easily have played the course in different ways at the start so that the third hole developed over time.

The top of the pigtrail looked out over a ravine—mucky wetlands fringed with rushes and fed by a small creek beside the second fairway. Montague, a connoisseur of the natural drainage of his land and its diversity of soils, would have appreciated this natural hazard. Beyond it, Keller and Cupp saw a landing area on the other side, about 110 yards away, which could have been the third green.

Standing there, looking back, they felt even more certain that they had been correct, for now another playing option asserted itself, provoked by the shape of the land. The Oakhurst players could have chosen to vary the play on different days, hitting two drives from the number-three tee—one ball to the third green, and one to the slope beyond, played as the drive for number four. The ravine, then, would have been a double-duty hazard.

Cupp knew that this doubling practice was common in the early days of golf and often used in Scotland, so the premise was not far-fetched, given what the land itself seemed to be saying. On the other hand, Cupp wrote in his journal, "Number four could also be played as a fairly short shot along the slopes with the tee to the left of number three green. The slope is tough, but it is up to the right, the best stance for a ball beater."

Cupp and Keller could feel by walking that the shorter version of number four would still have been a strenuous golf hole, complete with blind landing area for the drive. Given the potential of the clubs in the Oakhurst era, a tee shot would have hit the fairway above the slope, but from there it was still uphill, a forty-foot grade in all, 300 yards from tee to green.

As Keller and Cupp walked from the proposed number-four tee box up what would have been the fairway, the land offered clues to its history. The level area of what they assumed was number-four green was not visible from the tee, but a hint of the fairway line could be seen in what would have been exactly the right place. In the era of Oakhurst Farm, this had been known as the upper field, and the hill rose sharply upward to the right. The horses hadn't ventured up the hill, instead grazing what had once been fairway, neither flat nor dangerously steep. As Cupp put it, "The horses actually helped keep the fairways—or at least what had been fairways at the time of Montague—halfway between modern rough and modern fairway."

From the vantage point of what Keller and Cupp thought was the fourth green, and the highest point at Oakhurst Links, the view is, and would have been, breathtaking. Seven hills roll unbroken across the landscape, their woods the texture of gently brushed wool, and the golf course fills the sumptuous open space in three distinct tiers. Montague and company had taken the course from its logical start at the clubhouse, down through the first two holes, and then ingeniously maneuvered play all the way to the peak, less than halfway through. From there, the fifth hole could only have gone all the way down to the flat bottom field, a drop of approximately a hundred feet.

Cupp wrote of the drive from number-five tee, "This is a spectacular tee shot off the hill." The teeing area was more or less obvious, given its proximity to the fourth green, as it must have shared the small flat area. Keller and Cupp assumed that two good shots would have taken a player to the green on the lower field, and they guessed at where the fifth green had been placed, based on what they calculated would be a reasonable distance of about 175 yards. They also assumed another pigtrail had to have been there to enable the players to scramble down the steep bank.

From the fifth green, however, the course's layout was anything but clear, for several options for width and length were possible across the broad expanse of the bottom field. Obviously, the rest of the course had to fit in here, even if they had somehow guessed wrong about the previous five holes. Keller and Cupp decided to work backward from givens they had—the clubhouse and Cary Montague's assertion of hole number one. They also knew number nine naturally would have taken the players back to the porch, though their current guess at number two also lay more or less at the feet of the clubhouse and might have been the finishing hole.

Somehow the four remaining holes, whatever their numbers, had been carved out of what Oakhurst Farm had used as middle and bottom pasturelands. They wound in some fashion around what had been the horse barn, but to determine their layout, Keller and Cupp needed an anchor.

At this point Keller remembered with exhilarating clarity the discovery he and Lewis Jr. had made almost thirty years earlier, when they had come upon and tried to dig up the old golf cup, only to have the the rotting metal crumble at their touch. Keller recalled, too, the spot where they had made the discovery, straight down the hill from the clubhouse. To a golf course archaeologist, a disintegated golf cup was an irrefutable placement clue. What Keller and his son had always called "the green" was the one indisputable putting area on the bottom and middle fields. It could not have been the ninth green, for it was too far from the clubhouse, nor could it have been one of the starting holes, for in no logical way did it connect up to what they knew to have been number one. They guessed it had been number eight, and worked backward from there. This made design sense, as two of the earliest British golf course architects, H. N. Wethered

Lewis Keller restoring the eighth green.

and Tom Simpson, expressed it: "To think of a hole at golf is rather like thinking of a comet, with the head where the green lies and the tail streaming behind until it fades away at the teeing ground," adding, "The green is the point from which the hole springs."

In this location, the hole that the green suggested brought the course a natural and efficient symmetry. From the green, Cupp could visualize where the eighth tee must have been, back across the bottom field, close to what they had fixed as the fifth green. He could also discern where bunkers must have been placed. Of eight, he wrote,

[143]

This tee shot would be similar to, but the reverse of, number two tee shot, up over the slope left of the trees with the bunkers imbedded in the depressions in the slope short of the tee shot landing area. This could be a par five, but we did not hit the tee shot to see how far it would go. This seems as though it should be a large green like number one because of the open area and the ease of construction. There may have been a caped fairway bunker left of the second leg that might also be visible from the tee. This is an excellent match for the second hole with its bunker right of the second leg. Also two is short and dangerous with the creek while eight is long and open, requiring the player to work the ball close to or over the various bunkers in order to attain an advantageous angle to the green. The surrounding forms suggest the green could have been quite large with two bunkers. The bunkers would be highly caped to match the one in the fairway.

Locking number eight into place proved to be the critical breakthrough for the rest. Given eight, six and seven then came easily into view, and Cupp and Keller could now see these holes because they knew what to look for.

Keller and Cupp envisioned number six, placing the tee near to what they were confident was the fifth green, aiming back toward the clubhouse along the lowest part of the bottom field. Regarding the placement of six, Cupp wrote, "This hole could play 265 yards from the far corner to the green. . . . it's a very nice setting for a green with trees on the backdrop, though they would have to be limbed up for some sunlight to the putting surface. We have no real indication this may have been a green, but the landforms to the north look like a tee. Since the soils are very good in this area, the green may have been very flat and formless."

The fairway for six brought the player into position to head back on number seven. Six and seven would then have perfectly parallel fairways, taking up most of what had been the bottom field. In restoring number six green, which sits behind parapet bunkers with high capes, Cupp also relied on several photographs of similar greens of the era.

❧

SEVEN WAS THEN SKETCHED IN, based on how a logical next hole would have played. Cupp noted playing on the reverse axis of six, the tee opened beautifully onto a rolling portion of land identified by depressions on the left side. Crossing the fairway just beyond the landing area was a gentle swale, and the green became obvious on the far bank—very close by the fifth green and sixth tee complex. The putting surface became obvious as we rolled back the existing sod. There was also little doubt that this general area would also have been the location of eighth tee, and though there were no obvious land forms, the hillside gave all the clues.

Now Cupp and Keller were ready to pace out number eight, working their way forward from the seventh green up to "the green." One hundred and thirty yards wide, dappled with bunker humps that Cupp later honed into boiler pots, number eight emerged as one of the course's finest holes. It made sense of the rest of the course and led Keller and Cupp to the doorstep of the remaining, but crowning, achievement—the ninth and finishing hole.

Given the location of eight, the only conceivable placement for nine was as a crossover hole, the ninth fairway crossing the second, another example of land economy. Crisscrossing was common in golf courses of the Oakhurst era, the Old Course at St. Andrews had two and as Oakhurst Links was a private course, there would have been no other players to wait for, no wayward balls from another foursome to duck. As Cary Montague's own description of his father's golf course had noted, "Flat land is not plentiful in the Big Draft, and the course had to crisscross considerably to get enough flat spaces for the greens." A crossover here made perfect sense and enabled Keller and Cupp to twist the fairway slightly right, then left up the hill. It meant they could position the ninth green just at the foot of the Oakhurst porch—where it naturally would have been.

Cupp enthused in his journal, "The tee shot would be from directly behind the eighth green. It works pretty well up the slope and will definitely play as a par four. There were a number of depressions on the slope facing the tee and most had sandy residue, so we assumed they had been bunkers. The fairway is domed and difficult but a well-struck shot placed the player in perfect position for the uphill approach to the green. It was only necessary to level the green enough to make it puttable."

The result of this understatement proved to be magnificent: a green that was visible uphill from the tee, but had to be approached with both conviction and enough touch not to fly the green and break a window in the Oakhurst farmhouse. It was a classic finishing hole.

The last piece of the puzzle snapped into place, and the only piece of open land not accounted for by a golf hole was the small area where Montague had kept his cows.

Bob Cupp observed that "once the elements of the course were discovered there are some very attractive golf shots. It seems the game has always been meant to be played over and around objects of varying size and form and often close to or over peril or difficulty."

His reasoning bore out the notion that any good golf course should offer an innate narrative. A golf course is more than just a collection of golf holes end to end, nor do good golf holes simply lie down next to each other like knives and forks in a silverware drawer. Hole to hole, the course should unfold to the player as any good story unfolds, with an opening scene, suspense, and denouement. Thus the designer must also have the touch of a skilled narrator, as if planning to watch as every game plays out. Even though no actual drawings or plans of the Oakhurst layout survived—if indeed any had been drawn by Montague and friends—the sensibility of the Oakhurst founders clearly matched that of the best designers, and Cupp was able to discern their likely intent because their feel for this particular piece of land mirrored classic concepts.

Along the way, he and Keller applied their knowledge of soil science. Cupp and his team pulled up pieces of sod to study areas where the coloration of the soil changed. They could see from manure breakdown that the soil had been fertilized in certain places. Horticultural history also came into play, as Cupp recalled: "We even found some interesting species of turf, including some Colonial Bentgrasses that were known to be growing at the time."

Ever looking for more clues to support their proposed layout, Keller and Cupp were delighted when they reviewed Russell Montague's irrigation journal. No farmer, Montague had nonetheless tried to learn all he could about the science of land. His journal is the only true record of the landscape history of Oakhurst to survive, since it had stayed in the house. The book, barely larger than the palm of a hand and meticulously written, at first seemed to have nothing to do with golf, for not a word about the game or the golf course can be found there. Yet it revealed an invaluable clue.

An original piece of Russell Montague's irrigation pipeline system.

Russell Montague had been fixated by irrigation and how water traveled through soil. Among his many observations is a treatise titled "Fifteen Reasons to Drain Soil," which includes the following: "It carries off stagnant water and gives a ready escape to the excess of rainfall; it arrests the ascent of water from beneath, whether by capillary attraction or the face of a spring and by doing this it enables us to regulate the supply of water to growing plants." In sum, "Draining is indispensable as a preliminary step to all of the land improvements." Montague wrote in the journal of the importance of irrigation pipeline, then made of ordinary brick clay.

[149]

Russell Montague's original irrigation journal.

In the 1880s, when hoses and water pressure and irrigation systems were unknown, knowing the path of rain and groundwater would have been essential. It would have been especially important to carry runoff naturally by gravity to areas that needed water to preserve them, like putting greens and fairways, or away from others lest they grew too soggy for the ball. Thus one of the great coups of the restoration came when Keller and Cupp literally stumbled upon remnants of clay pipe in the bottom field after they had completed their layout of the holes. They felt this had to be a bit of Montague's original irrigation pipeline system, and sure enough, it led directly to the area containing the fifth and seventh greens. As Cupp described in a letter to a friend in Scotland in 1994, "Imagine how good we felt when we surmised holes five and seven only to find an old irrigation line leading to them."

While Keller and Cupp would spend some time redeliberating the sequence of holes, they were soon convinced that the layout that had come to them was the original Oakhurst plan. They had made a few design decisions—omitting a few bunkers, placing number four tee, laying out number six green—but all were based on their golfing instincts.

Cupp was satisfied that if Russell Montague and company could see the restoration, they would recognize the work as the original, and that he and Keller had gotten as close to Oakhurst Links as anyone could. "Though I knew academically how the game was played," he said, "I had now visited the past."

❧

IT NOW REMAINED to physically reconstruct the course. Each feature Cupp and Keller had sited was marked out with stakes so as not to be lost again. Cupp's team brought in new topsoil where needed, reworking the subsoils as close to the original composition as possible, and hand-shaping and building up the soil forms, mainly for the greens and bunkers, then planting grass seed. William Fuller, an expert soil agronomist who had worked with

Cupp for many years, was put in charge of bringing the reimagined holes back to playable form.

Replicating 1880s tee boxes was a far simpler task. To "tee" the ball meant to set up your next shot, and the 1775 rules stated, "Your tee must be upon the ground." Rubber tees in relatively modern shape came into existence in the 1890s, and were then superseded by wood. But originally a tee was merely a handful of sand pinched from a bunker or a bucket of sand placed by the tee area. There would also have been a bucket of water so that players could dampen their fingers and shape the sand into an elevation that would support the ball. Eighteen buckets, nine for sand and nine for water, completed the tee areas.

Meanwhile, Rosalie Keller supervised the creation of a clubhouse to serve as check-in area, pro shop, and Oakhurst museum. In the 1970s she had bought a used post office counter made of oak and hand-restored the wood herself. She had situated it as a bar in the family's den, but the post office counter now became the player sign-in desk.

A bibliophile, Rosalie tracked down copies of Margaret Montague's books, placing them between bookends in the entry hallways. The Kellers rearranged the library areas to incorporate the artifacts they had found, such as the golf ball John Keller had unearthed in his fossil hunt, another Oakhurst-era ball found during the restoration, and other photographs Dick Taylor and Lewis Keller managed to find. The original portrait ensemble of the

Layout of Oakhurst.

founders remained in the front hallway. No one knows what occasion prompted them to have their portraits taken, but Lionel Torin went all the way to Richmond to sit for his at a studio long since defunct. Montague and company looked down undisturbed on the rooms they had frequented more than a century before.

꿁

OAKHURST LINKS WAS reinaugurated on October 20, 1994, in a special event to coincide with the playing of the Solheim Cup at the Greenbrier. A large contingent was on hand, including the entire Keller family, Bob Cupp, and Karsten Solheim, the creator of Ping golf clubs. A corps of golf press covered the event, including writers from Scotland and Europe.

The primary celebrity, though, was Sam Snead. Wearing a lemon yellow sweater against the fall chill with his signature straw hat, he remained an icon of golf at age eighty-two. He was also, of everyone gathered, the pivotal character. Had he not felt like trying to take a few dollars from a newcomer with a fluid swing at the Greenbrier decades earlier, he would likely never have spoken a word to Lewis Keller. And had Keller not met Snead, Oakhurst Links could have passed from Cary Montague's hands out of existence forever.

Snead had been asked to take the first swing on

*Sam Snead and Karsten Solheim at the reinauguration
of Oakhurst Links.*

Oakhurst Links in more than a century. He teed up on
sand, on the short third hole. To celebrate the event, Solheim had insisted on providing Snead with a special club,
a one-of-a-kind marriage of old and new. To a solid hickory shaft of the original Oakhurst period, Solheim had
had affixed a high-tech head, finished in high-gloss black.
Snead examined the club and took a few easy swings, as
awe-inspiring as an octogenarian as Keller remembered
he was as a rookie. All eyes fixed on the golf great as he
prepared to strike an 1880s gutta-percha ball across Montague's ravine.

[155]

Sam Snead teeing off at the third hole.

Snead took his backswing slowly and then hit the ball, but even in the hands of a player of Snead's unfailingly graceful tempo, high-tech and hickory refused to marry, after all. The onlookers were stunned to see the head of Snead's golf club flying dismembered in the air, rising higher even than the guttie golf ball it had struck. The hickory shaft had snapped under the weight of the metal head and Snead's follow-through. Both ball and clubhead flew up and over the marsh.

The mishap didn't ruffle Snead. He quipped to all assembled, "Did either of 'em get on the green?"

9

THE ECHO OF MANY LANDSCAPES

BIG DRAFT ROAD REBUTS all change of mood, though it was widened in the 1970s to accommodate two lanes of traffic, putting travelers in more danger than in Montague's day. Drivers misinterpret the smooth macadam to mean it is safe to speed over the curves, but the drop-off is still fifty feet, still unguarded. Speed on Big Draft Road is as out of place as titanium golf clubs are at Oakhurst Links.

Half a mile up, a branch climbs off to the right, marked McCloud Road—the Americanized spelling—a record of the time when paths and wagon trails were named for the people who lived where the thoroughfares came to an end. MacLeod Road had carried Rod and Alick to the very top of Bob's Ridge, there to overlook

Oakhurst from their farmhouse, long since fallen down, but once close enough for them to walk in the evening light down to Montague's fireplace.

A mile farther, in the middle of a sharp uphill curve, lies Greycliffe, once the home of George Grant, still standing and regal. Three seasons of the year, the curtain of leafy woods obscures all but the tops of two redbrick pillars at the entrance of the drive that winds down to the house. In winter, though, with the leaves stripped away, the large brick manor with its steep gabled roof and circular entranceway is unmistakable, though no one who knew George Grant has lived there since the turn of the twentieth century. A dozen large oak trees march across the adjacent field, perhaps the grove that lent Montague's land its name.

Past the trees, the road flows over the rolling Greenbrier hills, the sunlight an uncanny tease of bright and shade. Montague Drive begins just before the church with the pews carved by Fraser Coron's knife from West Virginia hardwood, and proceeds past a "Children on Horses" sign, a caution from the days of Oakhurst Farm, up a rise, and across a bridge over Dry Creek.

The sign announcing Oakhurst Links is modest. Huge white pines, planted by the Montagues, line both sides of the lower driveway. Farther up, a next generation of pine trees has been planted by the Kellers.

Suddenly, ahead and to the left, the golf course comes

*From the driveway: The second tee and fairway,
with the fourth fairway uphill beyond.*

into view. Without players, it is not bold to the eye, except for the knot of tawny sheep moving lazily in unison, unhurried and unbothered, across the fairways. Even the quiet churning of a lone automobile in the gravel driveway seems alien and too modern a sound. To arrive at Oakhurst Links is to behold for all intents and purposes the year 1884.

❧

THE REBORN OAKHURST is both summation and starting point. The 9-hole, 2,235-yard, 35-acre golf course has never felt the swing of a modern golf club. The dizzying array of club choices that face the modern player—clubface size, whip of shaft, groove, material, brand name—are unknown here. The challenge of Oakhurst is the challenge of vintage tools and vintage ideas.

Masterfully made replicas of Oakhurst-era hickory-shafted clubs are virtually indistinguishable from the implements that would have once been in the hands of the original players. Lewis Keller's commitment to an authentic restoration for modern players had to include these, since the course made no playing sense otherwise. There would be no point to graphite shafts, and forged steel, and 300-yard drives on this golf course, where the longest hole is only 356 yards and meant to be played as a par five. Modern clubs at Oakhurst would be an unfair match of eras, and the real test is to meet Oakhurst on its own terms.

Lewis Keller remembered well the conversation he had with the handyman at Oakhurst, just after he had bought the property: "He told me that each player in those early days had six clubs. Three of them had wooden heads: the driver, the brassie, and the spoon. There were three iron clubs as well: a cleek, a sand iron, and a putter. All of the clubs had long heads and heavy shafts. No one had a bag in those days either. You just carried your clutch of clubs in your hand."

To re-create these conditions as closely as possible,

Keller sought out a maker of authentic clubs and found Millar Low in—not surprisingly—St. Andrews, Scotland. Low is a wiry man who has been playing golf himself for sixty years. His small shop in suburban St. Andrews gives no hint of the ancient work going on inside, the only metal in evidence that of the modern machinery, which whines enough to demand earplugs for all who step inside.

Most conversation here turns on the soft terms of wood—its "return" and "give," its overall forgiveness. The club makers speak with Low and his business partner, Vicki McNaughton, also a keen player, of shaping shots as if golf clubs in the hands of golfers are tools in the hands of sculptors. The fine subtleties of Low's Oakhurst clubs begin their lives locked in a block of wood. Even after the first exploratory trims have been sliced away, a needlenose clubhead, made of beech or persimmon, still starts out resembling a gnarled arthritic foot. The grain lines are visible all right, but there is no hint in the beginning of target spot, sweet or otherwise.

Low imports persimmon and hickory wood from the United States, including from the Southeast, and it is tempting to think that trees growing in Oakhurst's vicinity may provide some of the wood that reaches his shop. He hovers around the workers like a fatherly golf guru, certain in his belief that a well-made hickory shaft is as strong as any early steel shaft would have been. Clubs are made one at a time, the curve in the joints worked until it is silky.

Clubheads are sanded and filed to fabriclike smoothness, for the lacquer finish will pick up any scratch and accentuate any flaw left on the wood. The stains are as thick as syrup, in dark oak tone or light mahogany, and applied with fine brushes and polished to gloss with chamois cloth. Low's club makers regard the many honeyed tones of finish they use as their palette, paints to be dabbed and tried and buffed until they achieve the ultimate hue.

Light reflects the woody tones through the workrooms, bathing the entire operation in an amber glow, room to room, as lathes spin shafts, and chips and flakes of wood fly. The fragrance of fresh wood dust hangs in the air.

Lead is used to weight the finished clubs ever so marginally. An inlay of soft ram's horn is fitted on the leading edge of the clubface; grips are made of sheepskin and suede. In the 1880s a wax finish was traditional, and so all clubs destined for Oakhurst get this signature treatment.

Everything proceeds by eye, hand, and touch, and the club makers are likely more intimate with the meaning of their work than the players who will eventually swing the clubs, for here the object is conceived only for perfect outcomes. The clubs that leave Low's shop to emerge in the Oakhurst club room defy the experience of any modern golfer.

Keller went to similar lengths to get the Oakhurst

replica golf balls just right. Not only do they have to play like an 1880s ball, they also have to be gentle enough not to break 1880s replica clubs, yet strong enough to withstand day-to-day use.

Millar Low knew most of the companies active in the replica trade, and he suggested Keller contact the Penfold Company in Birmingham, England, which produces knickknacks and historic golf artifacts. As it turned out, Penfold still had a few molds from the 1880s that it used for making commemorative gutta-percha balls and museum models. It was the only company Keller could find that had the potential to produce Oakhurst golf balls in the volume he would need.

The challenge was assuring authenticity and uniformity. No one in the world had ever ordered 1880s golf balls in bulk to be played in the 1990s. Penfold sent Keller a few of the replica balls they'd been making up until then. The first time Keller hit the Penfold copy with a hickory club, all he felt was a dead clunk on the clubhead and no spring off the clubface.

What Keller needed was a quality control test team, and he called upon his son, grandson, and friends, including Gardner Dickinson. Penfold sent Keller some samples made from a different compound, a mixture Keller suggested of gutta-percha and balata, a sap from the same tree family. Keller believed balata would add strength, since the first batch of Penfold's pure guttie balls had, true to history, also cracked and split during play.

Each compound mix purportedly offered different speed and distance potential, based on different "compression," which in the case of these antiques meant how densely packed the compound had been.

Penfold produced a half dozen test balls, which Lewis Keller and his lab team tested on ranges and at the Loxahachee Club in Florida. According to Keller, this first batch flew too far for the historic period in question, even allowing for the fact that Keller and friends were well-above-average players.

A second batch was produced and sent to Keller, but when he and his friends played the revised balls, they were even more lively. They traveled about five yards farther on each shot than the first batch, roughly 170–180 yards with a vintage driver. Keller felt that was too far for an average 1880s player, given the Oakhurst layout, but he told Penfold in a letter, "The balls feel wonderful when struck with our hickory sticks and the scoring is equally as nice."

Penfold reworked the compression, and produced a few new samples. Keller and his friends and family tried them again, and found that this time Penfold had hit the right proportion of density and air. The balls now flew 100 yards with a mid-iron and 155–162 with the driver, just about the distance to a desirable first lie on the opening hole at Oakhurst.

Penfold replica guttie ball.

Until roughly the end of the nineteenth century, gutties had been all handmade, though still at a fraction of the cost of the feathery. But in the 1880s, when the original Oakhurst Links was launched, industrial-volume molds had been invented. Some were still available at the Penfold Company, but the only ones that had survived in Penfold's hands were molded to create a lattice pattern on the ball. Thus, all Oakhurst replica balls would have to be latticed, rather than individually nicked, as they would have been in the 1880s. These Penfold molds have been used to make each batch of Oakhurst golf balls.

❧

WHILE THE OAKHURST CLUBS seem familiar enough, it is hard at first glance to take them as friends. The needlenose driver of the 1880s looks exactly like its name: The clubface is long and horsey and, in its narrowness, seems unlikely to ever connect with a golf ball, let alone advance it any distance. The putter looks enough like the driver to be easily mistaken. The lofted iron and driving iron more resemble the club profile to which modern golfers have become accustomed. However, the rut iron looks more like a long-handled spoon, its beautiful brass orb clubface no larger than a silver dollar.

The rut iron was intended to advance a golf ball out of a wagon rut. However, in the hands of a modern player, it will more than likely produce a choppy divot, for the hand-eye coordination required for such minuscule striking surfaces defies any modern standard.

In actual Oakhurst play, the golf ball is enveloped by grass kept at the height that sheep will nibble, in the fairways sometimes high enough to sweep the shoelaces, and in the rough at times high enough to hide shoes altogether. Modern greens are layer cakes of sand, gravel, and seedbed, but the greens at Oakhurst have no such support underneath, no agronomical buildup nor hidden perforated drainage pipes nor engineered calculation. They are spongy underfoot with a putting surface kept at three-eighths of an inch, compared to one-eighth on an average

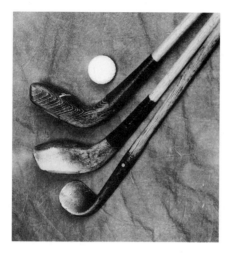

Vintage driver, rut iron, and putter.

recreational green or even shorter under the slick putting conditions of tournament play. The Oakhurst greens re-order a sense of touch and speed: It may take a ball as long to reach the hole from ten feet as it takes to walk off that same distance.

Golf at Oakhurst Links is entirely removed from the game all modern golfers carry in their bag and their head. It provides a sensation familiar but not quite known.

Graceful shots are at first hard to come by for players unaccustomed to hickory clubs, since the tendency is to swing too hard to compensate for the oddness of the im-plements rather than letting the clubs do the work. Yet

The fourth green and fifth tee, the highest point on the course, with the fifth and seventh greens far below.

there is a special exhilaration when one succeeds with wholly unfamiliar tools, for the golf of Montague's day defies false promises, and playing at Oakhurst strips away the pressure to keep up with the latest technology and the performance expectations they raise.

Unlike the Montague era, when the founders apparently played year-round, golf at Oakhurst Links today is played only from roughly May 1 to the end of October. During the off-season Mark Waid, Oakhurst superintendent, repairs the fragile replica clubs, which often break from the hard-swinging play of modern golfers. Waid can replace a piece of a chipped clubhead if he has the chip of

The Oakhurst clubhouse and gardens today.

wood, using liquid wood filler. But two types of repair are more common—replacing the weight in the clubhead, and fixing a split shaft. If the lead weight of a needlenose driver has come out, Waid pours a new one, using a sheet of lead flashing heated in a cast-iron pot suitable for cooking what amounts to lead soup. Once the lead has melted, Mark spoons it into the cavity in the club with a cast-iron ladle. After it cools and hardens, the repair is complete.

Mending the hickory shaft requires unwhipping the club, gently extracting the split pieces, fitting a new shaft into the clubhead, and rewhipping it. Waid spends hours each winter mending equipment, an heir to Fraser

Coron and the history of club making deep in the Oakhurst hills.

It is the middle of May before the flower beds can be stripped of the blanket of mulch that protects them during the winter. Rosalie Keller oversees the gardens, a rotating arrangement of annuals, biennials, perennials, and shrubs. The largest is a raised bed of yellow marigolds, and it usually takes two days to carefully plant a pattern of blooms, which by midsummer have grown into a thick blanket of yellow. Many of the original Montague plantings, including boxwood, wild phlox, violets, and jewelweed, were preserved by the Kellers to surround the clubhouse and museum.

In spring, local oral historian Martha Asbury takes up her role as clubhouse concierge. This includes taking players and visitors on tours of the clubhouse and museum, and outfitting players with their "implements of murder," plus two Oakhurst gutties, and a hand towel to wipe the sand from their fingers at the tee box.

The sheep return to the course each April 15 from their winter home in Lewisburg. Oakhurst has a flock of thirty to forty sheep, and they are not at all decorative, so superintending the course at Oakhurst means knowing sheep habits. During the era of Oakhurst Links sheep were an important supplement to whatever maintenance equipment the founders had, and they remain so today.

Sheep need a lot of care. The superintendent's job includes supervising the shearing, and midwiving during the lambing period. Sheep have a high incidence of twins and triplets. The second season Oakhurst was open to the public, a ewe died, leaving newborn twins: Mark Waid and Lewis Keller carried the newborns in their arms up to the Keller cottage above the golf course, where Rosalie set up a nursery in the laundry room. The Kellers bottle-raised the lambs until they were old enough to rejoin the flock.

At about eight weeks of age, lambs get frisky, and they race around the golf course after each other, occasionally stopping at the greens to butt their heads on the short flagsticks. Montague and the other founders probably took a lead from Scottish courses in using short flagsticks that would withstand the constant battering of sheep, and these have been replicated today. The Pattison steel-springed flagsticks, a true innovation, were never deemed necessary at Oakhurst.

The grazing flock is picturesque, but the main reason they roam the course is to nibble the grass to golfable length. The sheep, helped a bit by mowers, keep Oakhurst fairways at about one and seven-eighths inches, compared to roughly five-eighths of an inch for regular modern fairways. Through the spring and into summer the grass is tender, and the sheep happily remain within the fairways, with no fences needed to keep them from moving off. As hot, dry weather ensues, the conditions bring on a dramatic change in sheep behavior. Lack of a modern watering system at Oakhurst causes them to look for more succulent greenery, and they like to; they dart into the gardens to snatch mouthfuls of flowers. To discourage the wandering sheep, Mark Waid was forced to run a low-voltage electric wire around each flower bed.

Occasionally the golfer ready to putt at Oakhurst will look down and spot some puzzling sights. Sheep urine leaves deep brown burn marks with which a modern course need not contend, and ovine footprints are as common as play itself.

It is not that the sheep graze the greens—they don't seem to have much of an appetite for the bent grass of the putting surface—but they do traverse the greens as they move from fairway to fairway, or when they are crowding each other out of the way for the pleasure of butting their heads or rubbing their backs on the flagsticks. With greens this soft, residual indentations can often stop a rolling golf ball. A two-hundred-pound ewe can leave a hefty impression.

Oakhurst's local rules, which mirror those of the previous century, offer no relief in this case; the only free lifts are from sheep castings.

Oakhurst manages on dew for fairway irrigation. When the fairways dry and harden, they offer a different dimension, and when the grass surpasses the sheep, a new challenge. The greens are slightly more pampered. Each morning they are washed with a garden hose to remove the fungus and organisms that can damage the sensitive putting surface, and each afternoon, to counteract the burning rays of the sun, the greens are rinsed off to reduce their temperature. In this way, in an era increasingly concerned with minimizing the environmental impact of golf courses, Oakhurst is the ultimate in low maintenance and low impact.

$$\text{\&}$$

LEE TREVINO PLAYED Oakhurst twice, in the mid-1990s, and he might not have broken fifty either time for nine holes if he had played a full round. Fresh from having made a video on golf history in Scotland, Trevino recognized the challenges inherent in old-style play and observed that he would have probably been a caddie instead of a player if he had had to contend with the skill demands of golf a hundred years ago.

Tom Watson also played some Oakhurst holes in 1995, content to fly a ball over the grazing sheep, who were oblivious to his presence or his fame. Then, on number nine, he had to halt his play until the sheep moved off the fairway, as they were blocking the view of the all-important approach to the final green. Watson's satisfaction grew with each successive hole: He had gradually picked up the essence of the swing of his forebears.

Tom Watson at Oakhurst with Lewis Keller.

The skill needed at Oakhurst is counterintuitive to that of modern golf, because it cannot be acquired in any other than this place. Oakhurst is simply the only chance in the world to play the remembered game.

To underscore the importance of this experience, accomplished players, collectors, and devotees of the early ways of the game gave birth to an annual competition at Oakhurst, the National Hickory Championship. The brainchild of Pete Georgiady, a golf writer and collector of antique clubs from North Carolina, the tournament calls to life one of Russell Montague's own reflections of Oakhurst-style golf, made in 1929, when he himself was

[174]

playing what we now know as the modern game: "There's a lot of difference between the golf we played then and now, but I think we had just as much fun."

The first tournament, in 1998, drew forty-two players from around the United States and Canada and established two divisions. In the Open Division, players could use wood-shafted clubs of any period. In the Historic Division, golfers could use only the wooden needlenose clubs of the 1880s, and the dress code was golf attire of the same period. The event subsequently became a modern-day rite of Oakhurst Links.

"The first National Hickory Championship is under way," announced starter Georgiady, on the flawless Allegheny morning that opened the tradition.

True hickory players thrive at Oakhurst, and Ralph Livingston from Grand Rapids, Michigan, is among the best. To prepare for the first Hickory Championship, Livingston scoured old golf photographs, picked out a stylish player, and then hired a tailor to copy the costume so Livingston could wear it at Oakhurst. The suit was so authentic, it had no pockets for tees or ball markers, since neither were used at the time.

Livingston had also become a student of golf technology and the history of its evolution. In fact, after playing golf for ten years, he switched to hickories exclusively. He used to be so intense before a round of golf, he would tighten up while putting on his golf shoes even before the

Lewis Keller, Randy Jensen, and Pete Georgiady.

round began. With hickories, he eliminated his expectation of what the club should achieve, and in the process cut his handicap in half.

Randy Jensen from Omaha, Nebraska, was the winner of the first National Hickory tournament in the Historic Division, shooting a phenomenal 152 for two eighteen-hole rounds. Still, even he was capable of hitting one of his shots on the second hole so errantly off-line into Oakhurst's indomitable rough that, at one point, eight people were helping him look for it. Of the experience of golf at Oakhurst Links, he observed, "In this place, with these clubs, you can see exactly what those first great players were up against."

Joe Heinzmann at the 2000 National Hickory Championship.

Brian Siplo, a golf collector, writer, and highly skilled player from Massachusetts, was also drawn to the tournament. By way of explaining why he was standing in the heat of summer sporting a shirt, tie, and woolen cap and pants, about to hit his first drive with a club someone once mistook for a weapon, he said simply, "The historic aspect of this course. For years, other places were thought to be the 'first,' and it's exciting to push back the known limit, like discovering an unknown Renoir."

❧

Second shot on the second fairway at the 2000 National Hickory Championship. Players in the background are on the first fairway.

GOLF COMES FULL CIRCLE at Oakhurst Links, though the course came and went and almost disappeared without a trace. Instead, if golf courses offer an innate story of discovery, the story unveiled at Oakhurst, shot by shot, is the story of the game itself.

The dismissive gentleman visiting the early Oakhurst players, who accused them of playing adult marbles, surely missed when he predicted, "It may be a fine game for a canny Scotchman, but no American will ever play it except Montague."

Acknowledgments
and a Note on Sources

WE ARE IN SOME WAYS indebted to all golfers, for the atmosphere of golf is very conducive to congenial questioning among the like-minded. Most especially, we thank Sam Snead for his welcome, the tour of his trophy room, and his unique memories of Oakhurst and his early golf days. We are grateful for Robert Cupp's support and goodwill. Katherine Prior, our research specialist in the United Kingdom, brought her considerable skill and initiative to bear and turned up information about the Oakhurst coterie that had never before been known. Robert S. Conte, historian of the Greenbrier, long interested in Oakhurst, has been of gracious fundamental help throughout. We also want to acknowledge the Phillips Patton family, through whose efforts the 1884 Oakhurst Links Foundation was established in 1995.

In researching this book, we consulted and reviewed all extant materials, but we are also glad to have added to the body of knowledge about Oakhurst. We conducted new research in Scotland and England, and met the relatives of Torin, Grant, and the

MacLeods. We were thus able to accurately piece together the lives of the founders after they left West Virginia. New documents came to light during our research, such as the Nathaniel Bowditch letter and the Torin and Montague genealogies, that had not been known or examined before by writers about Oakhurst.

In Scotland, we must thank Joanna Myrtle Torin, Lady Young, for taking the time to discuss her great-uncle and the great city of Edinburgh, as well as her golf historian friend, Pat Colledge. Robert Wilson of Wilson's Ceylon Teas was also very helpful on the Torin trail. We also gratefully acknowledge the hospitality of Norman and Caroline MacLeod, for the welcome to Dalvey; Major General George Grant-Peterkin, for the welcome to Grange; and his lovely mother, Mrs. Dorothea Grant Peterkin, for her kind hospitality in London. Joel Montague of Amherst, Massachusetts, and Ruth and Harry Montague of Brookline, Massachusetts, were of great and enthusiastic assistance in sketching in missing pieces of the Montague family narrative. Nathaniel Bowditch of Philadelphia provided important materials and advice. Millar Low and Vicki McNaughton, club makers extraordinaire, provided a warm welcome in Scotland, and delightful golf to boot. Greg Ramsay, whose family helped bring golf to Australia, was extremely helpful as we went about tracing Oakhurst roots in Scotland, including saving us from a flat tire and much lost time. Walden House in St. Andrews was a congenial base, with special thanks to Pat Ciesla and Doreen McGlashan for guidance.

In Morgantown, Christy Vernon, librarian in the West Virginia University Archives, helped us make the most of a marvelous state resource, which should be kept intact and available at all costs. The Harvard University Alumni Archives and Library were also invaluable, as was the Peabody Essex Museum, especially Jane Ward, Curator of Manuscripts. The North House Museum in Lewisburg

ACKNOWLEDGMENTS

and the public libraries in White Sulphur Springs and Ronceverte were also vital. Indeed, this book would not have been possible without specialized collections and their caring professional librarians, which only underscores the importance of strengthening the library sciences, resisting the trend toward reducing public library hours, and maintaining the principle of the public free library, even as we embrace the benefits of digitalization.

The Reverend Douglas Pitt, a friend of the Montague family, has been generous in sharing personal communications. On a personal note, we'd like to thank Richard and Elizabeth Walker and Terry Thompson for help, encouragement, and constant hospitality; Jack and Nancy Murdick for very reliable friendship; and Randy Johnson for his unconditional encouragement. All other friends and family who have put up with the demands and cantankerousness of the authors are also gratefully acknowledged.

We would like to specially mention Susan Rabiner, our agent extraordinaire, a true devotee of writers who saw a book in the rough, even though she's never hit a golf ball. Likewise our publisher, George Gibson, who nurtured the text and presentation as carefully as a tournament putt.

Finally, restored Oakhurst Links and the full record of its history would not exist without the thoughtful stewardship and ongoing support of Lewis and Rosalie Keller and family.

Bibliography

BARKOW, AL. *The Golden Era of Golf: How America Rose to Dominate the Old Scots Game.* New York: St. Martin's Press, 2000.

BRENNAND, TOM. *Dulwich & Sydenham Hill.* London: Dulwich & Sydenham Hill Golf Club, Limited, 1994.

BROWNING, ROBERT. *A History of Golf.* London: J. M. Dent & Sons, 1955.

CONLEY, PHIL, ed. *The West Virginia Encyclopedia.* Charleston: West Virginia Publishing Company, 1929.

CONTE, ROBERT. *The History of the Greenbrier: America's Resort.* Charleston: Pictorial Histories Publishing Company, 1989.

CORNISH, GEOFFREY. *The Golf Course.* New York: Rutledge Press, 1981.

DAVIS, WILLIAM H. *Great Golf Courses of the World.* Norwalk, Conn.: Golf Digest Press, 1974.

FERNANDO, PAM. *Nuwara Eliya Golf Club: 100 Years.* Nuwara Eliya: Nuwara Eliya Golf Club, 1989.

FORRES GOLF CLUB. *Forres Golf Club: Centenary Souvenir.* Forres: 1988.

BIBLIOGRAPHY

HAWTREE, FRED, ed. *Aspects of Golf Course Architecture, I: 1889–1924.* Worcestershire: Grant Books, U.K., 1998.

JARRETT, TOM. *St. Andrews Golf Links: The First 600 Years.* Edinburgh: Mainstream Publishing Company, 1995.

LAMONT-BROWN, RAYMOND. *St. Andrews Scotland.* Stroud: Alan Sutton Publishing, 1996.

LEYBURN, JAMES. *The Scotch-Irish: A Social History.* Chapel Hill: University of North Carolina Press, 1962.

MACDONALD, CHARLES BLAIR. *Scotland's Gift: Golf.* New York: Chas. Scribner's Sons, 1928.

MACKENZIE, ALISTER. *The Spirit of St. Andrews.* Chelsea: Sleeping Bear Press, 1995.

MONTAGUE, RICHARD. *History and Genealogy of the Montague Family of America.* Amherst: Williams Press, 1986.

WARD-THOMAS, PAT. *The World Atlas of Golf.* London: Gallery Books, 1976.

WETHERED, H. N., AND T. SIMPSON, *The Architectural Side of Golf.* Worcestershire: Grant Books, 1929.

Index